Hellenic Studies 74

EQUINE POETICS

Recent Titles in the Hellenic Studies Series

The Art of Reading
From Homer to Paul Celan

Masterpieces of Metonymy
From Ancient Greek Times to Now

The Aethiopis
Neo-Neoanalysis Reanalyzed

Kinyras
The Divine Lyre

The Theban Epics

Literary History in the Parian Marble

Plato's Four Muses
The Phaedrus and the Poetics of Philosophy

Plato's Wayward Path
Literary Form and the Republic

Dialoguing in Late Antiquity

Between Thucydides and Polybius
The Golden Age of Greek Historiography

Poetry as Initiation
The Center for Hellenic Studies Symposium on the Derveni Papyrus

Divine Yet Human Epics
Reflections of Poetic Rulers from Ancient Greece and India

The Web of Athenaeus

Eusebius of Caesarea
Tradition and Innovations

The Theology of Arithmetic
Number Symbolism in Platonism and Early Christianity

Homeric Durability
Telling Time in the Iliad

Paideia and Cult
Christian Initiation in Theodore of Mopsuestia

Imperial Geographies in Byzantine and Ottoman Space

Aspects of History and Epic in Ancient Iran
From Gaumāta to Wahnām

EQUINE POETICS

by
Ryan Platte

CENTER FOR HELLENIC STUDIES
Trustees for Harvard University
Washington, DC
Distributed by Harvard University Press
Cambridge, Massachusetts, and London, England
2017

Equine Poetics
   By Ryan Platte
Copyright © 2017 Center for Hellenic Studies, Trustees for Harvard University
All Rights Reserved.
Published by Center for Hellenic Studies, Trustees for Harvard University,
   Washington, D.C.
Distributed by Harvard University Press, Cambridge, Massachusetts and
   London, England
Printed by Total Printing Systems, Inc., Newton, IL
Cover Design: Joni Godlove
Production: Kerri Cox Sullivan

Library of Congress Cataloging-in-Publication Data

Names: Platte, Ryan, author.
Title: Equine poetics / by Ryan Platte.
Other titles: Hellenic studies ; 74.
Description: Washington, D.C. : Center for Hellenic Studies, 2017. | Series:
   Hellenic studies ; 74
Identifiers: LCCN 2016057533 | ISBN 9780674975705 (alk. paper)
Subjects: LCSH: Horses in literature. | Greek poetry—History and criticism.
   | Horses—Greece.
Classification: LCC PA3021 .P53 2017 | DDC 881/.0109—dc23
LC record available at https://lccn.loc.gov/2016057533

Contents

Acknowledgments

M<small>ANY INDIVIDUALS DESERVE THANKS</small> for helping me produce this work, some for their great personal support, some for intellectual support, and many for both. First I must thank Jessica, my wife, for her unflagging encouragement and for the patience that she showed during my many late nights and weekends in the office. I also owe a great debt of gratitude to friends and mentors who read and critiqued this work throughout its many stages. I thank my dissertation advisor, Olga Levaniouk, as well as Ruby Blondell, Richard Salomon, and Stephen Hinds for their help and supervision during the initial stages of this work. I also thank Yurie Hong, Roshan Abraham, and Robert Lamberton for their helpful feedback on individual chapters. I am grateful to Zoë Selengut not only for friendly support but for the editorial and bibliographical expertise from which this project has benefited. I also give special thanks to Leonard Muellner for the extensive feedback that he provided during the completion of this manuscript.

Finally, I express my enduring gratitude to the Center for Hellenic Studies for providing me the research fellowship, as well as encouragement, that was instrumental in the completion of this work.

Introduction

THE WORLD OF THE ANCIENT GREEKS did not arise *ex nihilo* but developed from earlier cultures, which are harder to evaluate because of their extreme age. The last century or more of research has, however, proven that most of the languages of Europe, the Near East, and India all descend from a common language, Proto-Indo-European (PIE), and that the various cultures of the Indo-European (IE) world, including the Greek, descend in some way from that of the speakers of that language. Although the world of the prehistoric IE peoples is very difficult to study, linguistic and archeological research allows us significant insights, and thanks to that research we know much more about the prehistory of Greek culture than we did even a short time ago. My intention here is not to contribute directly to that study itself, however, but rather to investigate certain facets of the earliest recorded Greek poetry in ways that draw on that research meaningfully and, I hope, innovatively. Specifically, my work is a literary analysis of the treatment of horses and horsemanship in early Greek poetry that incorporates elements of what has been revealed about prehistoric treatment of horses to explain unique and heretofore puzzling elements of Greek verbal art.

I begin this study with a review of Homeric equine formulas, focusing on ὠκέες ἵπποι. My analysis of the special position of this phrase in Homeric poetry grows out of an evaluation of our evidence for its existence in pre-Homeric poetry, from the distant ancestors of the Greeks to Greek poets who lived just before the advent of alphabetic writing. I work to show how certain prehistoric developments in the phrase affected its proliferation in Homer and to reveal its relationship to several seemingly disparate equine formulas. Chapter 1 concludes with a study of the word κλυτόπωλος, a somewhat perplexing epithet of Hades, the origin of which is, I believe, inextricably bound to the deep history of the these formulas, as well as the history of Homeric horse formulas generally.

In Chapter 2 I turn to horses themselves and to their relation to epic heroes. There I focus not only on the similarity of treatment accorded to them in epic verse but also on the fact that they share with humans a unique relationship to the gods: they can descend from the immortals, and they are capable of deriving semi-divine status from them. This extreme similarity of horses and humans, at a deeply ontological level, has parallels elsewhere in the IE world and reflects inherited ideology that ought to color our analysis of Homeric horses. I strengthen this assertion with a survey of evidence for horse sacrifices in the IE world that testify to a long tradition of thinking of humans and horses in uniquely similar ways.

In Chapter 3 I examine Greek lyric comparisons of horses and humans, which, unlike epic comparisons, often involve both male and female subjects and frequently have erotic overtones. After discussing the phenomenon itself I again turn to our evidence for horse sacrifices, which testify to a long cultural history of using horses to think about sex and power. I ultimately suggest that the sexual element of the symbology of the horse provides a key to understanding the metapoetic deployment of the image of the charioteer in Greek poetry.

Finally, in Chapter 4 I address the role of chariots in Greek and Indian marriage myths. This analysis reveals methodological distinctions between equine phenomena that are directly inherited from the parent culture and those that evolved independently but can still be meaningfully understood through an appreciation of inherited poetic practice.

Preliminary Evidence and Preliminary Assumptions: Horses and Proto-Indo-European Culture

My argument primarily concerns early Greek poetry, but it would be useful first to foreground certain key details about the study of horses that have been revealed in the fields of linguistics and archaeology. Horses and horsemanship have, in fact, long held a central position in investigations of IE history, especially those concerning the homeland of the PIE speakers,[1] and the justification for this position is vouchsafed by archeological, religious, and poetic evidence. There are, however, certain long-standing debates concerning whether

---

[1] For an extended review of these debates, see Drews 1988:121–57. For the issue of the Indo-European homeland see Mallory 1993. Although beyond the scope of this project, the field of genetics is bringing new perspectives on these subjects, using approaches that are so recent that they are not considered in most of the bibliography that will be cited in this work; see Haak 2015. Throughout this work I will be using the traditional term, Proto-Indo-European (PIE), to refer to the common language from which both the Anatolian and the non-Anatolian daughter languages descend. For the purposes of these arguments it may be considered essentially synonymous with other terms that have been proposed for the earliest reconstructible phase of the parent language, such as "Indo-Hittite" (Hamp 1990) or even "Proto-Indo-European I," proposed by Adrados (2007).

Indo-Europeans were the first to domesticate the horse, when this domestication occurred, to what purposes horses were first put, and what the significance of horse domestication is for an understanding of the Indo-European homeland and expansion. The difficulty of scholarly consensus on these questions need not preclude the present discussion, because my argument does not depend on any of the more contentious or uncertain elements of the subject.

The foundations upon which my work does stand should be made clear at the outset of this study. These assumptions are, I believe, beyond serious dispute and constitute sufficient basis on which to build an argument. The most elemental of these is simply that the PIE community was itself aware of the horse and that the horse was not individually encountered by each of the descendant IE communities in subsequent cultural phases as use of the domesticated horse spread throughout Eurasia. This assumption rests primarily on the linguistic evidence of a shared equine vocabulary among several descendant IE languages. The PIE $h_1ék̂uos$, 'horse', yielded Hieroglyphic Luwian *a-su-wa*, Sanskrit *aśva*, Avestan *aspa*, Tocharian A *yuk*, Tacharian B *yakwe*, Greek ἵππος, Latin *equus*, Venetic *eku*, Anglo-Saxon *eoh*, Gaulish *epo-*, and Old Irish *ech*, as well as Lithuanian *ashvienis* (stallion), Old Church Slavic *ehu-skalk* (horse-groomer), and Mitanni *a-as-su-us-sa-an-ni* (horse-trainer).[2] Had these cultures encountered horses individually, after the dissolution of the PIE community, they would have created their own innovative terms for the animal, which they did not do, or borrowed vocabulary from the same communities from whom they acquired knowledge of the animal itself. If they had borrowed this vocabulary, even if they had borrowed it from other IE languages, this would be clear linguistically. For example, the English word "marshal," descends from the borrowed Frankish word "marahskalk" and displays clear English phonetic development on top of old Frankish phonetic development. Hence, it is discernible as a borrowing, even though it was borrowed long ago from a related language. This is not the case, however, with IE equine vocabulary. These words, then, individually descend from the same PIE word, reconstructable as $*h_1ék̂uos$.[3] The simple presence of horses in the Proto-Indo-European society may, therefore, be taken for granted.

---

[2] See Mallory 1989:119 on these and other cognates. An extensive overview of what is known about the horse across the IE cultures may be found in Gamkrelidze and Ivanov 1995:463–479.

[3] It should be stated clearly that the Greek ἵππος is the most surprising of these forms and that its spiritus asper is still perplexing, but that its relationship to the same root as these other words mentioned is nevertheless clear, and fully supported by Mycenaean evidence. For the difficulties in its etymology, see Frisk 1960:1.733–5. Furthermore, work by A. Kloekhorst (2008:237–239) and by Michiel de Vaan (2009) suggests that the PIE antecedent of Greek ἵππος may, in fact, have been a *u*-stem noun rather than an *o/e*-stem as has generally been speculated and is assumed here.

The high status of horses in that society is also to be assumed, although I am aware that this assertion, despite its prevalence in scholarly tradition, lacks definitive archaeological verification.[4] Even without such archeological evidence, however, the likelihood of such a status is strongly suggested by such phenomena as the frequency of words for horse utilized in Indo-European personal names, such as Indic *Aśva-cakra*, Avestan *Vīśt-āspa*, Greek *Hippo-lytus* and *Phil-ippos*, Gaulish *Epo-pennus*, and Old English *Eo-maer*, to list but a few. There also exists a pair of so-called Indo-European Divine Twins, who are frequently and specially associated with horses and who appear in wide enough manifestation in the religious systems of Indo-European cultures to justify the assumption that the figures themselves, as well as their hippological associations, are of genuine Proto-Indo-European antiquity.[5] The Greek Dioskouroi (known as the λεύκιπποι, bright horses), the Anglo-Saxon *Horsa* and *Hengist* (Horse and Stallion), the Indic *Aśvins* (horsemen), and the Lithuanian *Dieva dēli* (sons of the sky) furnish the clearest evidence of this fact.[6] I believe that these facts render secure the assumption that horses were in the parent culture a symbol of high social status. Prehistoric Indo-European artistic treatment of horses is also remarkably consistent cross-culturally, especially in the particular treatment of horse heads and legs,[7] and the special place of horses in kurgan graves of the Yamnaya culture, identified by Gimbutas as an, if not the, early Indo-European people, may also lend credence to this assumption.[8]

Finally, the domesticated status of horses is assumed as well. The domestication of horses, at first as a food source and then for the purpose of riding, has been proven convincingly by Anthony.[9] He shows this through the age-slaughter patterns of horses evident at Neolithic sites; the consistency of age of death reflects the selected slaughter of kept animals rather than animals procured by hunting,[10] and he reveals evidence of bitwear in some horses as proof of riding.[11] This conclusion is strengthened by the presence of horse bones in kurgan graves alongside those of sheep and dogs, animals known to have been domesticated.[12] The Indo-European horse sacrifice, a kingship ritual which is documented in

---

[4] Fortson 2004:41–43; Mallory 1981: 205–226; cf. Anthony 1986.
[5] Mallory and Adams 2006:432.
[6] Fortson 2004:23–24. For special attention to the Baltic tradition and the ways in which it testifies to the deep cognition of the group see Frame 2009:72.
[7] Maringer 1981.
[8] Gimbutas 1997. It should be noted that Gimbutas's findings, although influential, have been widely criticized; cf. Mallory 1981.
[9] Anthony 2007:193–224.
[10] Anthony 2007:201–206.
[11] Anthony 2007:206–213.
[12] Mallory 1981.

Indic, Irish, and perhaps Roman sources, and which is widely thought to have been the principal PIE kingship ritual,[13] also requires a domesticated horse.[14]

A final set of concerns that often attend IE horse research regard the purpose to which these domesticated horses, provided that they were indeed domesticated, were put and, specifically, whether they were used as draught animals. The conclusion that the Proto-Indo-Europeans had wheels and wagons is rendered beyond doubt by the linguistic evidence: English *wheel*, Greek κύκλος, and Sanskrit *cakram* all derive from the same PIE word **kᵤekᵤlo-* (an apparently reduplicated nominal derivative of **kᵤel-*, 'to turn', perhaps connoting something like a "turny-turn," which perhaps reflects the repetitive nature of the thing described[15]). Additionally, Latin *rota*, Irish *roth*, German *rad*, and Lithuanian *ratas* all also mean 'wheel' and derive from the PIE root **ret-* 'to roll'.[16] The PIE root **ᵤegh-* yielded English wagon, Greek (ϝ)όχος, Latin *vehiculum*, Lithuanian *vežimas*, Sanskrit *vāhana*, and Avestan *vāsa*. The words axle and nave are also widespread and traceable to PIE.[17] Current archaeological evidence, however, does not permit the conclusion that horses were used in the drawing of these chariots, since no harness suitable for horses, rather than oxen, is known to have been invented before the breakup of the PIE speakers, however that event is to be understood or dated.[18] It is probable, then, that the domesticated horse was kept by the IE peoples for some time as a food and as a riding animal without being put to the harness. This assumption need not, however, have significant impact on the current discussion—most of the argumentation in this work deals with horses themselves and not with the chariots which they draw. When my argument does address charioteering itself, as occurs in the third and fourth chapters, I adduce what I think is a new argument, that poetic depictions of charioteers throughout the IE world evolve independently, and subsequent to

---

[13] This sacrifice is discussed at length in Chapter 2.

[14] The horse-training treatise of the Mitanni, although late, also warrants mention in that it proves that the Hurrians took their horse-training vocabulary from the Indo-Aryans and thus reflects a unique Indo-Aryan expertise in horse-training, which, in light of other evidence, reflects a genuinely ancient tradition. See Dent 1974. For text and commentary see Kammenhuber 1961.

[15] For a similar phenomenon, cf. Aristophanes *Frogs* 1313–4: αἵ θ' ὑπωρόφιοι κατὰ γωνίας / εἰειειειειλίσσετε δακτύλοις φάλαγγες; "[spiders] who in the corners under the roof tu-tu-tu-tu-turn the threads with your fingers."

[16] Rix and Kümmel 2001:507. Sanskrit *ratha* also descends from this word and has synecdochally come to mean "chariot." Pairs or groups of synonymous or nearly synonymous PIE words preserved severally in later languages are not unusual. For example, the triplet group, **man-*, **ᵤiro-*,* *ner-* (all roughly meaning 'man') yielded English man, Latin *vir*, and Greek ἀνήρ.

[17] It is interesting that these words are both metaphorical, meaning 'shoulder' and 'navel', respectively, a fact which has been seen to suggest that the devices were late inventions in PIE culture which attracted innovative names; see Fortson 2004: 38.

[18] Raulwing 2000:98–99; Anthony 2007:402–403.

the breakup of the IE community, but in logical and stable ways from treatments of horses that predate the use of the yoke.

In summary then, whether Indo-Europeans developed horse domestication themselves or acquired it from neighboring peoples, it is clear that they did employ domesticated horses at a very early period, and, regardless of the very first purpose to which horses were put (they were probably food before anything else), they were certainly employed before the breakup of the Indo-European speaking community.

Finally, as we turn our attention to the real subject of this work, the oral treatment of horses in oral Greek poetry, I should mention a potential complication that arises necessarily from my source material. This difficulty lies in the fact that many of my assumptions about prehistoric Indo-European poetic practice rely on evidence provided by Greek, Indian, and Iranian languages. The potential difficulty here lies in the fact that some linguists believe that these languages belong to a subgroup within the Indo-European language family, in other words, that they share a common ancestor that was itself a descendant of Proto-Indo-European.[19] If this is true then some of my assumptions about poetic practice in the parent culture would need to concern that common parent rather than the parent of the entire Indo-European language family. Even if that is the case it is not impossible for those conclusions to pertain to the culture of the speakers of Proto-Indo-European as well, but it would be difficult to verify. It would, however, only complicate some intermediate steps in my argument and would not alter the ultimate conclusions offered here regarding Greek verse.

[19] See Clackson 1994. Although Clackson ultimately argues against this view himself, his work is, to my knowledge, the most extensive study of the subject and contains the most thorough bibliography.

1

"Swift Horses" from Proto-Indo-European to Greek

HORSES ARE NEARLY UBIQUITOUS IN THE EARLY RECORDED POETRIES of the Indo-European world, and one particular facet of this presents a perfect starting point for our discussion: a reconstructible Proto-Indo-European poetic expression describing horses. For the earliest poetries of Greece, India, and Iran not only treat horses in ways that are strikingly similar but even utilize some of the same poetic vocabulary for describing them. In particular, horses in Homer are described with the phrase ὠκέες ἵπποι, "swift horses," while the Avestan Gathas use the corresponding āsauuō aspåŋhō, and the Sanskrit Vedas use āśavas aśvās.[1] All three of these descend directly from the same PIE phrase, *h₁ōk̑éu̯-es h₁ék̑u̯-ōs.[2] This shared history indicates that the phrase *h₁ōk̑éu̯-es h₁ék̑u̯-ōs is likely to have been in use in the poetry of the PIE speaking community and that the Homeric ὠκέες ἵπποι reflects a direct continuation of this prehistoric usage.[3]

---

[1] For the sake of enhancing the transparency of cognition, when Sanskrit phrases are to be compared to cognates I will provide the Sanskrit without sandhi (the phonetic changes that take place at word boundaries) and without phonetic change to consonants in absolute final position, whereby consonants are pronounced differently when they end a phrase). I will, of course, preserve all relevant phonetic changes when actual poetic lines are quoted. The dating of these literatures is of central importance to this sort of argumentation but, as with all oral poetry, is extremely problematic. The process of composition involved in all cases was very long in duration, but the linguistic eras represented principally by our surviving texts may both be safely assumed to predate that of the Homeric corpus (which will be considered the 8th century BCE). The compositional date of the Old Avestan corpus will be considered to be very roughly 1000–500 BCE; Beekes 1988:xi. The age of the *Rigveda* will be taken to be roughly 1500 BCE; Witzel and Jamison 2003:65.

[2] For further evidence of this see Schmitt 1967:238.

[3] For a similar conclusion from the point of view of our Sanskrit sources see Durante 1971:93.

This is not to say, of course, that PIE poetry deployed this phrase in precisely this form and precisely this order on all occasions, although it may be assumed that it did at times. As Edwards remarks in his criticism of this conventional understanding of formulas, a formula is not a thing "handed down over the ages, like a mummified cadaver, fixed in memory."[4] Instead, what are generally perceived as formulas, and will conventionally be called so here, are the results of oral compositional techniques which constantly and innovatively exploit thematic, phonetic, and metrical associations to facilitate composition in performance. These techniques, which may more truly than formulas be considered the inheritance of one generation of oral singers from another, render certain patterns as naturally, not prescriptively, frequent products of such composition. That is to say that the sorts of scenes and activities in which horses are likely to be mentioned will restrict the vocabulary items with which they occur and that the poetic devices employed within the singer's cultural tradition, along with the metrical restrictions of the poetic genre, will further facilitate certain associations of vocabulary which appear as formulas in the fixed and popular sense.[5] In some limited cases, such as Parry's famous noun-epithet formulas, specific coincidences of vocabulary are so frequent that they do genuinely function as bound units, but these are exceptional.[6]

$h_1\bar{o}k\acute{e}\mu\text{-}es\ h_1\acute{e}k\mu\text{-}\bar{o}s$ should not be imagined as the only PIE poetic expression for horses, but simply as the one that yielded ὠκέες ἵπποι, the prolific Greek equine formula. Yet this phrasing must have been used frequently in PIE poetry and the cultural and poetic pressures that caused this frequency must have been sufficiently continuous and long-lived for the constituent elements of this phrase to maintain a strong association into the Greek poetic period. Thus, the particular ways in which this phrase functioned in Proto-Indo-European and in Greek should be defined, as far as is possible, so that a comparison of these formulas may reveal how this maintenance of practice may be accounted for in light of the linguistic and poetic developments of the Greek epic, since these developments may be assumed to have eradicated many other PIE poetic features in the descendant traditions. Such an understanding will prove instrumental in our appreciation of early Greek poetic treatment of horses.

The importance of the horse to PIE as well as Greek culture indicates a continuum of horses' significance in the intervening phases between these two cultures, and the importance of speed to the horse's value is easily accepted.[7]

---

4   Edwards 1988:29.
5   Compare Watkins on formulas for "immortal fame," 1995:173–178; also Lord 2000:13–29.
6   Lord 2000:30–67.
7   For artistic documentation of the preeminence of horses in ancient Greece, see Markman 1943. For a survey of the economic and political significance of horses in Greece, see Camp 1998.

There would, however, certainly have been numerous ways to say "a fast horse" in Proto-Indo-European. Therefore, to establish that this particular phrasing is likely to have occurred frequently in PIE poetics, and that its appearance in Greek, Vedic, and Avestan verse is not simply coincidence, the phrase must be shown to exhibit poetic characteristics, as it does quite readily.

In fact, the phrase *$h_1ṓk̂e̯u̯-es$ $h_1ék̂u̯-ōs$ demonstrates several features of PIE poetic technique.[8] The consonantal sequence $h_1-k̂-u̯-s$ occurs identically in both words, forming an alliteratively bound pair.[9] The phrase seems, in fact, to form a jingle, and would presumably have been quite catchy to the ears of a PIE speaker.[10] Yet this phrase would, of course, have appeared in other cases, just as it does in the later traditions, and the phonetic correspondences manifest in the nominative would not be completely identical to those found in other forms. The accusative plural and genitive plural formulas, to draw examples from those occurring most frequently in Homer, may be reconstructed, respectively, as something like *$h_1ōk̂u-ms$ $h_1ék̂u̯o-ms$ and *$h_1ōk̂u-ōm$ $h_1ék̂u̯-ōm$. The basic schematic pattern of consonantal alliteration is maintained throughout all the cases, although the final consonant or consonant cluster in each is different; likewise the vocalic features retain poetic qualities in each case, but less neatly than in the nominative. Phonetics alone, then, support the possibility of this phrase having been poetically useful and, therefore, likely to have been deployed by the PIE poet. This evidence, taken together with the phrase's appearance in our three later IE poetic sources, supports the hypothesis that the later IE formulas descend from a genuinely PIE poetic phrasing.

There is, however, another, less obvious, poetic figure represented here, which makes this conclusion even more compelling. For the two words involved in *$h_1ōk̂e̯u-es$ $h_1ék̂u-ōs$ derive from the Proto-Indo-European *$h_1ék̂u̯o-$, 'horse', and *$h_1ōk̂u-$, 'swift', the similarities of which are immediately striking. As mentioned previously, the consonantal makeup of both words is identical. Additionally, the difference between the semi-vowel u̯ in the former and the fully vocalic u of

---

[8] Some of the ensuing analysis also appears in Platte 2014.

[9] The predilection of PIE verse for alliteration may be inferred from the frequency of this stylistic device in later traditions, but is also frequently revealed in PIE poetic reconstructions; cf. Watkins 1995:28–49. Watkins' *$égu̯hent$ $ógu̯him$ represents a similar alliteration of labiovelar elements, although voiced in this case, as well as a similar alternation in root vowel. It is also interesting to note that even in Latin poetics, an area in which innovations so readily obscure evidence of PIE poetic inheritance, alliteration in very early verse is quite common, as early Saturnian verse makes clear.

[10] My use of the word "jingle" is influenced by Watkins' usage. See, for example, Watkins 1995:328. For an overview of PIE poetic technique in general see Schmitt 1967, especially 221–284. For an overview of poetic technique with an eye toward Greek inheritance specifically see Durante 1971, especially the first volume.

the latter is simply the expected allophonic variation of the phoneme u in pre-vocalic and final position, which is to say they are essentially the same sound. The final o of *$h_1$ék̑u̯o- is simply the nominal suffix (o/e) used to form o-stem nouns, as in both the Greek and the Latin second declension. The principal difference evident in these two words, then, is in the central vowels, yet when one recalls that ablaut of e and o was a fundamental element of PIE morphology, even this distinction appears to be of superficial, derivational, significance. Therefore, the first of this pair of words is, probably, a suffixed noun of the same root of which the second word is a lengthened o-grade adjective. They seem to be a noun and adjective pair deriving from a common root *$h_1$ek̑-, and sharing the same base meaning, 'swift'.[11] These words would, therefore, form a *figura etymologica*, translatable as something like 'swift swifties,' akin to Greek, ἔπος ἐπεῖν, Vedic ávocāma vácaḥ, and Avestan uxδā vacā, all descending from the PIE *u̯eku̯os u̯eku̯, "to speak a speech."[12] Unlike those *figurae etymologicae*, the "swift horses" formula does not maintain its transparently etymological quality in the later traditions, but in the PIE phase of the language the phrase would have exhibited this pronouncedly enough to have been readily recognized by its hearers.[13] The distinctiveness of this highly specialized poetic feature along with the demonstrated artfulness of phonetic arrangement makes it highly likely that this phrase is the ancestor of Homeric ὠκέες ἵπποι.

"Swift Horses" in Greek

The fact that this PIE phrase is so unlike ὠκέες ἵπποι is paradoxically reaffirming. For ὠκέες ἵπποι is relatively devoid of obviously poetic qualities, especially in comparison to its cognates, Avestan āsauuō aspåŋhō and Vedic āśavas aśvās, despite the fact that it is more frequently utilized. One would, in fact, expect a reconstruction of its linguistically earlier forms to restore to the phrase some earlier poetic features. This sort of reconstruction is routinely utilized on a smaller scale regarding Homeric phrases with original digamma, such as ὀλίγον γόνυ γουνός, reconstructed as ὀλίγον γόνυ γονϝός so as to reveal an earlier and much tidier euphonic sequence (*Iliad* XI 547). Similarly we find ὠκέες ἵπποι

---

[11] Watkins 1995:23.

[12] The fact that these words formed a *figura etymologica* has been pointed out elsewhere: Katz 2010:361.

[13] These examples of later phrases of the ἔπος ἐπεῖν type do not reflect precisely the same sort of derivational relationship in their constituent members, but should not be expected to, as vowel ablaut was no longer active in the linguistic phases represented here. Nevertheless, a continuity of underlying practice seems evident. English "sing-song," although not historically traceable to PIE, demonstrates something slightly more akin to the PIE ablaut pattern represented here.

shortly after its loss of the digamma in ὠκέες (< ōkéu̯es), and the conversion of the labiovelar, the qu-sound, in ἵπποι (< hík̯u̯oi), which would have euphonically patterned with both the velar k-sound of ὠκέες and the labial semi-vowel sound of the lost digamma, and sounded something like ὠκέϝες ἵκϝοι.[14] Phonically then there is good reason for this pair of words to have maintained its close poetic relationship until a period only shortly before our Homeric verse was recorded, since the comparatively unpoetic appearance of ὠκέες ἵπποι would appear to be a very recent development.

However, even though the phrase had only recently changed at the period of the recording of our Homeric texts, it had changed nevertheless.[15] The fact that this phrasing was not finally lost at a point after the occurrence of these linguistic shifts and just before the period that was to be preserved in our textual tradition requires explanation. For just like historical and dialectical word forms, oral formulas should be employed only so long as they continue to be useful, which may indeed be a very long time depending on how each is individually affected by diachronic change. Poetic formulas then should not be expected to have been preserved simply for the sake of tradition, as oral poets are neither rigid conservators of poetic forms nor daring innovators, but rather practical craftsmen. They continue to use the words, formulas, and techniques which they inherit so long as a use can be found for these elements within the confines of their contemporary poetic systems, even if this is a new use. Therefore the poetic artfulness responsible for the early development of the poetic treatment of this phrase is only a partial explanation of its prevalence and persistence in Homer. It explains why the Greek oral poets would have inherited the phrase initially, but not why they would have preserved it and continued to use it after the occurrence of the linguistic shifts that permanently altered its poetic qualities. To understand this, one must examine the applications of the phrase in early epic itself.

The phrase occurs declined into nearly every case. The frequency of each case is charted below in Table 1.1. Although Iliadic uses dominate, and will receive most consideration here, I list all occurrences in Homer and Hesiod

---

[14]   I must make clear here that the word ἵππος may never have contained an actual labiovelar, but instead a velar followed by a labial, with a syllabic break occurring between the two sounds, that is ἵκ-ϝος rather than ἵ-κϝος. I am assuming here that the conversion of this consonantal group occurred at roughly the same time as that of the labiovelars. This should be a safe assumption since the two developments proceeded in much the same way. That the loss of labiovelar was a late development in Greek is guaranteed by its presence in Mycenaean Greek.

[15]   I do not consider the Homeric text to be a perfect preservation of any one moment of poetic-linguistic development, but rather the result of a more fluid and evolving oral and textual tradition that only became fixed as the current text late in its history. I will, however, treat our text practically as representing a broad period of poetic-linguistic development.

simply to provide a good impression of the phrase's proliferation throughout early Greek poetry. The symbol / indicates a line end, and ellipses mark wherever other words intervene between the two under consideration.

Table 1.1. Frequency of ὠκέες ἵπποι formulas

Phrase (basic)	No. of Occurrences in *Iliad*	No. of Occurrences in *Odyssey*	No. of Occurrences in the Homeric Hymns	No. of Occurrences in Hesiod
ὠκέες ἵπποι /	10	1	–	1
ὠκέες...ἵπποι /	1	–	–	1
ὠκέας ἵππους /	18	2	–	2
ἵππους / ὠκέας	2	–	–	–
ἵππων ὠκειάων /	2	–	1	–
ἵππων... ὠκειάων /	1	–	–	–

This formula system then seems to exhibit very regular behavior, as may not be surprising for one of such common use. The declensional distribution is in the normal pattern, as outlined by Hainsworth, in that the accusative is the most common, followed by the nominative, and then the genitive.[16] The dative and vocative forms are unknown, and the nominative and accusative formulas are the only ones that appear with any frequency. These two most common formulas also happen to be of the shape - ᵕ ᵕ - - and occur always after the diaeresis and run to the verse end, filling up the so-called adonean clausula. These forms then do make up something akin to formulas in the very rigid sense, much like Parry's noun-epithet formulas, and thus belong to a rather small network of such heavily regularized expressions.[17] Within this network, however, this phrase is not at all unusual, since most such phrases occupy this exact position. There is a strong incentive for the creation of rigid formulas at the end

---

[16] Hainsworth 1968:48.

[17] Due to their particularly regular deployment, formulas of this type were central to much of Parry's initial work, and have long exerted great influence on approaches to formulaic behavior as a whole.

of a poetic verse, especially in dactylic hexameter. Unlike the rest of the verse, in which permissible resolution in the arsis allows the occurrence of either a long syllable or two short syllables, the sixth foot of a line of dactylic hexameter is formally bound to be spondaic. The fifth foot is slightly freer, in that resolution is still technically possible, yet so bound in practice that fifth-foot spondees are rare. Thus phrases of this metrical type, $-\smile\smile--$, were extremely prone to this sort of regularizing, so long as their sense was useful. The phrase ὠκέες ἵπποι, given its especially desirable metrical characteristics and semantic suitability to heroic verse, was particularly fit for this sort of regularizing, as unusual as this development may be within the more general practices of oral poetics.[18]

Thus, although the date of the beginning of dactylic hexameter verse, a Greek innovation, is debated,[19] it should nevertheless predate the phonetic evolutions that permanently altered the appearance of this phrase. There is good reason to think that this phrase had attained prominent formulaic status in Greek heroic verse before the alteration of its originally inherited phonetic and poetic character. By the time of the transformation of the characteristics that had once preserved this expression, other uniquely Greek uses adhered to the phrase. I assume that during most of its life it behaved as most poetic expressions do, as words loosely associated by phonetic, metrical, and thematic pressures so as to appear together frequently, but not in any one consistent position or orientation. This was probably true at the point at which dactylic hexameter verse developed among Greek-speakers, after which the idiosyncrasies of this new meter occasioned a tendency for this phrase to appear at line end and in one particular order, thus elevating it to the realm of truly regular formulas. The prominent position to which this expression had risen may have been sufficiently powerful to contribute to its preservation in the Greek oral poet's vocabulary despite changes in its phonetic nature. It is interesting to note that this phrase's Sanskrit and Avestan counterparts, although still alliterative, are not as regularized in position. The deployment of the phrase in Homer is anomalous, but it may be this very anomaly that best testifies to the utility of the phrase and best explains its proliferation and longevity there.

Beyond a phrase's linguistic and metrical assets, however, may lie more literary qualities which also contribute to its proliferation, as is especially true here. For even a very metrically useful formula should not be expected to have

---

[18] This formula is largely restricted to the *Iliad*, where horses appear much more frequently than in the *Odyssey*.

[19] See Nagy 1974.

been preserved solely for the sake of occupying one position, but may have developed uses dependent on cultural and artistic resonance, and one of these may actually be particular to highly recognizable formulaic units such as this. Once even limited regularity of deployment develops, this may itself propel the formula into genuine prominence, necessarily imbuing the phrase with new literary potential, since these rigidly bound formulas acquire allusive capabilities. Such development is clearly present here, as an overview of the deployment of the nominative case alone illustrates. The nominative formula occurs ten times in the *Iliad*, and two of these appear in identical lines in book XVI, at line 383 and 866: ἵετο γὰρ βαλέειν· τὸν δ' ἔκφερον ὠκέες ἵπποι, "for he longed to strike him, but his swift horses bore him away."[20] Although these lines are not in extreme proximity to each other, they are close enough to have featured in the same performance and so might seem like a purely mechanical result of oral composition—in other words, this line was fresh enough in the poet's mind that he simply reused it to provide himself time to plan the next lines. Yet the second occurrence does more than simply fill space, representing as it does the deliberate deployment of a poetic device. The first of the two lines occurs at the beginning of Patroclus' aristeia at the moment when, carried away by his seemingly superhuman, nearly Achillean, prowess, he desires to kill Hector and storm Troy himself. The second appearance occurs just after Patroclus has died, as Hector, finished boasting over the corpse, tries to catch Automedon, who has taken the horses of Achilles from Patroclus. The line then is the same, but the referents have changed: 383—"for he [Patroclus] longed to strike him [Hector], but his [Hector's] swift horses carried him [Hector] away"; 866—"for he [Hector] longed to strike him [Automedon], but his [Automedon's] swift horses carried him [Automedon] away." Hector has transformed from pursued to pursuer, has taken the place of Patroclus as doomed hero, now tragically chasing his own death.

It is also important that the first use of this formula refers to Hector's horses, but recalls the verses about Achilles' horses that precede it:

...ὠκέες ἵπποι
ἄμβροτοι, οὓς Πηλῆϊ θεοὶ δόσαν ἀγλαὰ δῶρα.

...the swift horses, the immortal ones which the gods gave to Peleus as glorious gifts.

Iliad XVI 380–381

---

[20] All textual translations are mine unless otherwise noted.

The verses that follow this are repeated after the final occurrence of the formula as well, and in fact end the book:

ἵετο γὰρ βαλέειν· τὸν δ' ἔκφερον ὠκέες ἵπποι
ἄμβροτοι, οὓς Πηλῆϊ θεοὶ δόσαν ἀγλαὰ δῶρα

for he longed to strike him, but his swift horses carried him away, the immortal ones which the gods gave to Peleus as glorious gifts

Iliad XVI 866–867

Although the formula itself, ὠκέες ἵπποι, remains the same, the greater semantic units that it anchors have been rearranged to highlight the dramatic shift that has occurred in the narrative. The irony of the fact that the immortal horses of Achilles could not catch the horses of Hector has given way to the sudden impotence of Hector and the ineluctability of his impending fate, for with the death of Patroclus the dramatic action of the *Iliad* switches to Hector's own death.

This formula, furthermore, has a particular association with Hector. Of its ten occurrences in the *Iliad*, four have to do with him, and the only repeated extended formula based on the nominative ὠκέες ἵπποι is Ἕκτορος ὠκέες ἵπποι (VIII 88, XVI 833). In addition, a full half of the occurrences of the ὠκέες ἵπποι formula appear in book XVI. Book XVI develops this association between Hector and the formula ὠκέες ἵπποι, and manipulates its contextual significance in service of the work's greater narrative structure.

One final point to be considered is that the second occurrence of this extended formula immediately follows the lines αὐτίκα δὲ ξὺν δουρὶ μετ' Αὐτομέδοντα βεβήκει / ἀντίθεον θεράποντα ποδώκεος Αἰακίδαο, "then with his spear he immediately pursued Automedon, the godly servant of the swift-footed [Achilles] son of Aeacus" (XVI 864–865). Achilles, the figure whose impending return has informed this entire formulaic discourse, is finally linked to this formula explicitly. For although Achilles himself is not yet present, his formulaic epithet is joined to the ὠκέες ἵπποι formula by their common element, the adjective ὠκύς, "swift," which appears in both of the epithets most common for Achilles: as the second element of the compound ποδώκης, "swift-footed," and as an independent adjective in πόδας ὠκύς, the uncompounded form of the same phrase. The valor of horses connotes the valor of the horses' heroic owner,[21] and it is no coincidence that the salient feature of the formula designating valorous horses finds its second most frequent expression in formulas attached

---

[21] Cf. the βραδέες ἵπποι, "slow horses," of Nestor, who has grown too old for combat, to be discussed in Chapter 2; *Iliad* VIII 104.

to Achilles. The changing role of Hector has been dramatized by the changing semantics of the ὠκέες ἵπποι formula, and now, as this formula's newest application foreshadows Hector's impending demise, it echoes the Achillean epithet so as to foreground the epic's ultimate hero, whose preeminence will occupy the remainder of the work. Book XVI consistently reinforces the association of Hector with this "swift horses" formula but ultimately reminds the audience that Hector's heroism will soon give way to that of Achilles. The frequency and prominent position of this formula render it more exploitable in the intersections of formulaic and narrative technique, thus providing a new mechanism by which the phrase maintained and even expanded its position in Greek epic verse.

The extent of this application, however, is not limited to strict reiterations of the formula, but also encompasses modified formulas, the significance of which is influenced by the frequent and maintained use of the base formula. Modification of the nominative, ὠκέες ἵπποι, occurs once in Homer and once in Hesiod, and does not initially appear to be a modification of this formula at all, but of the secondary formula ἵπποι...ὠκύποδες, "swift-footed horses." The Hesiodic use of this formula may indeed be treated as a modification of this derivative formula system,[22] but the Homeric occurrence is best understood within the ὠκέες ἵπποι system and may indeed serve as a useful link between these two. The Homeric formula occurs in the chariot race of book XXIII: φαίνετ', ἄφαρ δ' ἵπποισι τάθη δρόμος· ὦκα δ' ἔπειτα / αἳ Φηρητιάδαο ποδώκεες ἔκφερον ἵπποι, "suddenly the pace of the horses was stretched to the utmost and then quickly the swift-footed mares of the son of Pheres bore him off" (XXIII 375–376). Although we have the compound ποδώκεες rather than the familiar ὠκέες, when the line is considered from only the fourth foot onward, it will be noted that -ὠκεες ἔκφερον ἵπποι is simply a reversal of the first two words of the extended formula already mentioned: ἔκφερον ὠκέες ἵπποι. It will also be noticed that there occurs, in the line immediately preceding this, the word ὦκα, "swiftly," in precisely the same metrical position that would normally be occupied by ὠκέες. Thus, a sufficient number of the expected elements of the ὠκέες ἵπποι formula is present for these lines to be evaluated as a reorganized expression of this basic formula.

An explanation for this unusual structuring may, at least initially, be sought within the mechanics of oral verse composition. This line's first four feet, which belong strictly to the previous sentence, involve the word ἵπποισι, "horses" in

---

[22] I say this only because, in Hesiod, formulas of the "swift-footed horses" variety are preferred to the simple "swift horses" formulas favored in Homer, so within the confines of Hesiodic verse one may prefer to analyze this formula within its own system.

the dative plural. It would have been irregular to fill the last two feet of the verse with the normal nominative formula because that would have caused unusual repetition of the noun. Yet the formula, being in the mind of the poet, may still have provided a model for the last two feet of the verse, as indicated by the preservation of the word ὠκύς in adverbial form and perhaps by the phonetic resemblance in the replication of the unvoiced labial stop, the pi, of ἵπποι in ἔπειτα. Thus, one of the vocabulary elements of the base formula is preserved in addition to the formula's signature phonetic sequence, and with this formula so phonetically present in the last two feet of line 375, the poet may have been disinclined to use it in the same position so soon afterward in line 376. Instead, the poet created a seemingly unique formulation based on the models presented by these two other derivative formulas, that of the Hector and Patroclus episode and the ποδώκεες extensiions (discussed below) to convey the essential idea.[23] Thus, this formulaic deviation may paradoxically be conditioned by the regularity and commonality of the basic formula.[24]

Yet this modification also highlights a shift in the formula's semantic import, as becomes clear when considered in the light of the following line: αἱ Φηρητιάδαο ποδώκεες ἔκφερον ἵπποι / τὰς δὲ μετ' ἐξέφερον Διομήδεος ἄρσενες ἵπποι, "[suddenly the pace of the horses was stretched to the utmost and then quickly] the swift-footed mares of the son of Pheres bore him off, but the stallions of Diomedes bore him on after them" (XXIII 376–377).[25] The poet seems at this moment to be very concerned with highlighting the distinction in gender between the two groups of horses. In all of Homer, the definite article is used with the "swift horse" formulas only this one time. It is important to note that Homer regularly uses masculine forms of ὠκύς in these expressions, even when female horses are involved. Genitive plural forms are an exception and will be discussed shortly. There is also no specific word for "mare" in Greek (the word ἵππος is simply accompanied by a feminine form of the definite article, or the phrase θῆλυς ἵππος, "female horse," may be used[26]). It is therefore difficult for the poet to specify that the horses under discussion are either male or female, and it is

---

[23] Given the paucity of our sources, we cannot be certain that this formulation was not more common than our one preserved occurrence would lead us to believe. However, even if other examples did occur, as may be likely, they may still be understood within the model offered here.

[24] These formulaic modifications do not have to be seen as derivatives exclusively, but may draw on the same sorts of phonetic, metrical, and thematic associations that occasioned the creation of the early freer formulaic networks out of which the later rigidly bound use developed. Yet even if this is the case, given the regularity of the final formula, this modification must be synchronically informed by the ὠκέες ἵπποι formula even if both descend, to some extent, from common practices diachronically.

[25] Cf. Hainsworth 1968:94.

[26] Cf. *Iliad* V 269.

apparently rarely of concern to do so. This unique definite article, however, does distinguish the horses as female, and its prominent positioning does so quite dramatically. These particular horses, in fact, are gendered not only here but in their first mention in the catalogue of ships, when they are modified by the feminine adjective ἄρισται (II 763). These horses are apparently noteworthy in their gender, for reasons that I will discuss below, and the poet is being careful to highlight this fact. The formula ὠκέες ἵπποι did not need to be divided in order to include a definite article, but the marked innovation in such a standard formula draws special attention and therefore serves to spotlight the poet's effort.[27] Finally, it is worth noting that this gendering of the horses may even be employed to occasion something of a sexual pun in the next two lines that would be dependent on a *double entendre* for the verb ἐπιβαίνω: Τρώϊοι, οὐδέ τι πολλὸν ἄνευθ᾽ ἔσαν, ἀλλὰ μάλ᾽ ἐγγύς· / αἰεὶ γὰρ δίφρου ἐπιβησομένοισιν ἐΐκτην, "those [male horses], the ones of Trojan birth, were not far behind, but very close, for they always seemed about to mount the chariot" (XXIII 378–379).[28] The potential for nonformulaic horse expressions to derive meaning from formulaic expressions testifies to the fact that ὠκέες ἵπποι, despite its change in phonetic character, attained a literary status which developed from, and reciprocally maintained, its formulaic prominence.

I would like to move now from the usage of the nominative forms of this phrase to an analysis of the usage of the genitive and accusative. I do this in part for the sake of thoroughness, to offer the reader a full survey of the Homeric artfulness represented herein. I also hope that in the course of this, however, I will build an impression of a marked tendency for rather extreme phonetic patterning in and around these expressions, which will be relevant in analysis of other, related equine formulas at the end of this chapter.

In moving to the genitive formula, ἵππων ὠκειάων, we see another example of explicit equine gender, and although this version is relatively rare, it is still quite fascinating in its formulaic behavior. It occurs only twice in unmodified form, but presents a unique deviation from the other formulas in that it is reversed in word order, and fills three feet, an entire half of a line. One possible explanation for the reversal in word order may be that in this particular version the phrase takes up more space than it does in its other cases: it extends beyond the diaeresis that generally defines these formulas, and which may be the

---

[27] Once the decision had been made to begin the line with the article, there may also have been a tendency to move one part of the upcoming formula into greater proximity to it.

[28] On the sexual usage of ἐπιβαίνω see Liddell 1996:624, sub voce AIII3. Aristotle uses it of quadrupeds generally: ἐπιβαίνοντος ἐπὶ τὸ θῆλυ τοῦ ἄρρενος, "with the male mounting the female" (*History of Animals* 539b26). Compare the double meaning of ἐπεμβάτης in Anacreon's famous lyric about the Thracian girl, to be discussed in Chapter 3, pages 74–76.

principal force determining the shape of most verse-end formulas. Although both the adjective-noun possibility and noun-adjective would scan identically, and would occupy the same space in the line, the adjective-noun formula would have obliterated this diaeresis, while the noun-adjective leaves it intact.

This conclusion seems to be confirmed by another formula entirely. The only other occurrence of the word ὠκειάων in Homer is in the formula νηῶν... ὠκειάων, "of the swift ships," which appears twice: νηῶν ἐπιβησέμεν ὠκειάων (*Iliad* VIII 197); νηῶν ἐπιβαινέμεν ὠκειάων (*Odyssey* ix 101). These formulas, νηῶν ὠκειάων and ἵππων ὠκειάων, would have scanned identically, and in both examples the adjective, ὠκειάων, occurs at verse end. The conventions of diaeresis may have rendered the formulas ὠκειάων ἵππων and ὠκειάων νηῶν equally undesirable and given rise to the word order in both cases. It is also noteworthy that these, again, are explicitly female horses. Yet, unlike the previously mentioned female horses, the gender of these particular horses does not seem to have special significance. In this case, the feminine form of the adjective seems to have been preferred because the usual masculine form would not have scanned in dactylic hexameter.

Finally, just like the nominative, the genitive formulas also exhibit a modification by separation, although only in one instance: Δεξιάδην ἵππων ἐπιάλμενον ὠκειάων "[he threw his spear at] the son of Dexias as he jumped upon his swift mares" (VII 15). The purpose for this deviation from formula does not seem to be the highlighting of any narratological oddity, nor does any metrical consideration necessitate the separation of the adjective and noun, as Δεξιάδην ἐπιάλμενον ἵππων ὠκειάων would scan perfectly well. Perhaps this modification was made instead to reflect the dramatic action of the line by presenting words that seemed to be jumping from their place just as the character involved jumps upon his horses. Thus end the rare genitive forms of the "swift horses" phrase.

The most interesting phenomena, however, belong to the accusative formula, ὠκέας ἵππους, and these will lead us to an analysis of these formulas' poetics in general. The accusative phrase generally occupies the same position in its verse as the nominative, but appears twice with modification by verse-end separation:[29]

ἐξῆγεν πολέμοιο δυσηχέος, ὄφρ' ἵκεθ' ἵππους
ὠκέας, οἵ οἱ ὄπισθε μάχης ἠδὲ πτολέμοιο
ἔστασαν ἡνίοχόν τε καὶ ἅρματα ποικίλ' ἔχοντες·

---

[29] For a full discussion of the mechanics of verse-end separation, see Hainsworth 1968:105–109.

[Polites] led him away from the grueling war, until he came to the swift horses which awaited him away from the battle and war, those which had a charioteer and chariot beautifully wrought.

Iliad XIII 535–537

χερσὶν ἀείραντες φέρον ἐκ πόνου, ὄφρ' ἵκεθ' ἵππους
ὠκέας, οἵ οἱ ὄπισθε μάχης ἠδὲ πτολέμοιο
ἕστασαν ἡνίοχόν τε καὶ ἅρματα ποικίλ' ἔχοντες·

[his comrades] lifting him in their arms, bore him away from the struggle, until he came to the swift horses which awaited him away from the battle and war, those which had a charioteer and chariot beautifully wrought.

Iliad XIV 429–431

The two appearances of this modification introduce the same repeated lines. Similar examples of runover epithets have been studied by Bassett,[30] who showed that they are used to form a bond between one idea and another, preceding one. I suggest that this particular example demonstrates a further purpose. These lines describe two separate, but very similar scenarios: both depict wounded heroes being helped to their horses by a comrade in order to flee from a fight which they cannot win. The fact that the person aided to his horse in the second example is Hector (the first is Deiphobus) also demonstrates a continuity of application in that it parallels the allusive manipulation of the nominative phrase, used specifically to dramatize Hector's dramatic arc. It seems that the expected formula shape may have been avoided in order to draw attention to the unusual ignominy of the act depicted and to provide a device by which these two scenes could be linked. The deviation from the expected formula shape draws attention to the unusual event being described, and this modified formula is then exploited for its own allusive potential, which is nevertheless still dependent on the unique status of the base formula.

The preservation of this formula despite fundamental alterations to its phonetic structure is understandable on literary as well as metrical grounds. Yet the loss of certain sorts of phonetic artistry ought, in common formulas, to give rise to new varieties, which reinforce the formula's newfound prominence. Further investigation into the deployment of the accusative case of the ὠκέες ἵπποι expression demonstrates that such new phonetic associations did indeed develop. The accusative case, ὠκέας ἵππους, is even more heavily regularized

---

[30] Bassett 1926.

than the nominative, so is a particularly apt subject for this sort of investigation. It is, in fact, so regularized that even three of its extensions attain formulaic status themselves: ἔχον ὠκέας ἵππους; ὑφ' ἅρμασιν ὠκέας ἵππους; ἐλαύνομεν ὠκέας ἵππους. A truly unusual regularization of the phonetic patterns around the phrase, however, shows the persistence of the dental nasal, the *nu*, immediately preceding the formula in nearly every occurrence:

> *Iliad* III 263: τὼ δὲ διὰ Σκαιῶν πεδίον δ' ἔχον ὠκέας ἵππους
> *Iliad* V 240: ἐμμεμαῶτ' ἐπὶ Τυδεΐδῃ ἔχον ὠκέας ἵππους
> *Iliad* V 261: ἀμφοτέρω κτεῖναι, σὺ δὲ τούσδε μὲν ὠκέας ἵππους
> *Iliad* V 275: τὼ δὲ τάχ' ἐγγύθεν ἦλθον ἐλαύνοντ' ὠκέας ἵππους
> *Iliad* VIII 254: εὔξατο Τυδεΐδαο πάρος σχέμεν ὠκέας ἵππους
> *Iliad* VIII 402: γυιώσω μέν σφωϊν ὑφ' ἅρμασιν ὠκέας ἵππους
> *Iliad* VIII 416: γυιώσειν μὲν σφῶϊν ὑφ' ἅρμασιν ὠκέας ἵππους
> *Iliad* X 527: ἔνθ' Ὀδυσεὺς μὲν ἔρυξε Διΐ φίλος ὠκέας ἵππους
> *Iliad* XI 127: εἰν ἑνὶ δίφρῳ ἐόντας, ὁμοῦ δ' ἔχον ὠκέας ἵππους
> *Iliad* XI 760: ἂψ ἀπὸ Βουπρασίοιο Πύλονδ' ἔχον ὠκέας ἵππους
> *Iliad* XII 62: ἀφραδέως διὰ τάφρον ἐλαύνομεν ὠκέας ἵππους
> *Iliad* XV 259: νηυσὶν ἔπι γλαφυρῇσιν ἐλαυνέμεν ὠκέας ἵππους
> *Iliad* XVI 148: τῷ δὲ καὶ Αὐτομέδων ὕπαγε ζυγὸν ὠκέας ἵππους
> *Iliad* XVII 465: ἔγχει ἐφορμᾶσθαι καὶ ἐπίσχειν ὠκέας ἵππους
> *Iliad* XVIII 244: χωρήσαντες ἔλυσαν ὑφ' ἅρμασιν ὠκέας ἵππους
> *Iliad* XXIII 294: διογενής, ὑπὸ δὲ ζυγὸν ἤγαγεν ὠκέας ἵππους
> *Iliad* XXIII 516: ἀλλὰ καὶ ὣς Μενέλαος ἔχ' ἐγγύθεν ὠκέας ἵππους
> *Iliad* XXIV 14: ἀλλ' ὅ γ' ἐπεὶ ζεύξειεν ὑφ' ἅρμασιν ὠκέας ἵππους
> *Odyssey* iii 478: καρπαλίμως δ' ἔζευξαν ὑφ' ἅρμασιν ὠκέας ἵππους
> *Odyssey* iv 28: ἀλλ' εἴπ', ἤ σφωϊν καταλύσομεν ὠκέας ἵππους

The only two exceptions occur at V 275 and X 527, and line V 275 can readily be accounted for as a modification of ἐλαύνομεν / ἐλαυνέμεν type of formula seen in XII 62 and XV 259. The anomaly of line X 527 occurs within the much-disputed Doloneia, which is notorious for its unexpected diction and syntax, so does not detract strongly from the appearance of a genuine poetic habit.[31]

Thus we have seen the formula expand to encompass not only the fundamental semantic unit, the basic accusative formula, but also to influence elements that are phonically regular, but semantically unrestricted. Furthermore, the regular extended formula, ἔχον ὠκέας ἵππους, involves additional phonetic attraction in that the phase is always preceded by a voiced dental, a delta: δ' ἔχον ὠκέας

[31] A wide-ranging study of the idiosyncrasies and possible origins of the Doloneia can be found in Danek 1988.

Table 1.2. Frequency of related dual formulas

Formula	*Iliad*	*Odyssey*	Homeric Hymns	Hesiod
ταχέ᾽ ἵππω	2	–	–	–
χαλκόποδ᾽ ἵππω	2	–	–	–

ἵππους (III 263; XI 127); Πύλονδ᾽ ἔχον ὠκέας ἵππους (XI 760). A slightly altered version of this also appears in Τυδεΐδῃ ἔχον ὠκέας ἵππους (V 240). Although extra-formulaic features may be of obvious utility in helping a poet structure a line which he knows will end with a common formula, it is unclear at the moment why these particular examples were so regularized. The *delta* and the *nu* are homo-organic in articulation, so there may have been a quasi-alliterative quality to this composition, and the *nu*, coming as it does before an initial vowel, may have its origin in a moveable *nu* that was extended to wide distribution through the mnemonic demands of the craft and performers' own poetic sensibilities.

In addition to the extended phonetic artistry of the formula there is extra-formulaic metrical consistency. The foot preceding ὠκέας ἵππους is dactylic in all but two instances: the already irregular V 275, in which the use of the dual may help explain the exception, and XVII 465. There is a nonessential but broadly consistent extra-formulaic metrical component to the deployment of this formula. Finally, although the Homeric and Hesiodic treatments of horse formulas often differ slightly, it is interesting—if admittedly potentially coincidental—that these two practices are also preserved in Hesiod: ἡνίοχοι βεβαῶτες ἐφίεσαν ὠκέας ἵππους and Κύκνε πέπον, τί νυ νῶιν ἐπίσχετον ὠκέας ἵππους (*Shield* 307; 350). Although these phonetic patterns may appear trivial, they seem to reflect an unusually strong tendency toward phonetic patterning in and around these formulas, perhaps influenced by the sheer frequency and regularity of their usage.

To see the true extent and significance of this patterning, however, we must now turn to dual formulas. The phrase ὠκέες ἵπποι does not actually occur outside of the plural. The absence of the singular is interesting but not completely surprising, since horses most frequently appear in teams and only rarely is an individual horse called to the audience's attention. The absence of duals is, however, more surprising since chariots could indeed be pulled by a pair of horses, and pairs of horses are mentioned as normal in Homer.[32] Isolated dual formulas, semantically related to the ὠκέες ἵπποι formulas, do occur (see Table 1.2).

[32] See Delebeque 1951:143.

Table 1.3. Frequency of related plural formulas

Formula	*Iliad*	*Odyssey*	Homeric Hymns	Hesiod
μώνυχες ἵπποι /	8	–	–	–
μώνυχας ἵππους /	25	1	–	1
καλλίτριχες ἵπποι /	3	–	–	–
καλλίτριχας ἵππους /	8	3	1	1
καλλίτριχε...ἵππω /	1	–	–	–
χρυσάμπυκας ἵππους /	1	–	–	–
χρυσάμπυκας...ἵππους /	3	–	–	–

The expression ταχέ' ἵππω, "fast horses," is essentially synonymous with ὠκέες ἵπποι, and χαλκόποδ' ἵππω, "bronze-footed horses," although not synonymous, does describe the horses' feet, calling to mind the formula πόδας ὠκὺς Ἀχιλλεύς, "swift-footed Achilles," as well as κύνες πόδας ἀργοὶ ἕποντο, "swift-footed dogs followed," so both may be considered related to ὠκέες ἵπποι.[33] The most interesting element of these substitutions is their phonic correspondence with the principal expression, in their preservation of the unvoiced velar, the *kappa*, of ὠκύς, once with the corresponding aspirated counterpart, a *khi*, and once as the identical unaspirated velar of ὠκύς in echo of the initial aspirate. Although ὠκύς itself does not appear in the dual, maybe a simple fault of our sources, these formulas clearly reflect it phonetically.

The assertion that these dual formulas, ταχέ' ἵππω, and χαλκόποδ' ἵππω, are meaningful phonic responses to ὠκέες ἵπποι may seem untenable, based as it is on only one corresponding consonant. There are several other formulas that do not as fully accord with ὠκέες ἵπποι semantically, but are nevertheless extremely useful for comparison (see Table 1.3).[34]

---

[33] For the mechanics of synonymic substitution in Homeric formulas, see Paraskevaides 1984. It is very interesting that in the two occurrences of the phrase, χαλκόποδ' ἵππω, it is immediately followed by the word ὠκυπέα at the start of the next line: VIII 41, XIII 23. It seems that even without a dual form of ὠκέες ἵπποι to deploy, the phrase itself is still somewhere in the mind of the poet, conditioning a bond between the two words that runs across the line boundary: χαλκόποδ' ἵππω / ὠκυπέα.

[34] Μώνυχες and ὠκέες are the two most common epithets of horses in Homer (Delebecque 1951: 149).

These formulas, combined with ὠκέες ἵπποι and its inflected counter-parts, comprise a list of the most common formulas involving horses in Homer, and every one of them displays an unvoiced velar, of either the *kappa* or the *khi* variety, at the beginning of the syllable preceding ἵπποι, just as the dual formula ταχέ' ἵππω does, and indeed they often precede that velar with another at the beginning of the word, just as the dual formula χαλκόποδ' ἵππω does. Admittedly, the formula χαλκόποδ' ἵππω does not exhibit the velar in precisely the same position as the other formulas, but, in light of the other evidence, it may be considered to belong to the same nexus of phonic and semantic formulation. It seems then that the network of Homeric horse-formulas is influenced by the association between the word ἵππος and the unvoiced velar, for which the most obvious explanation is the prominence of the word ὠκύς in the formulaic system. We then have a phrase that is not simply a common element in epic diction independently, but that is part of an entire network of phonetically and semantically related phrases.

The fact that these unvoiced velars seem to serve as the obligatory counterpart to ἵπποι may descend from the consonantal phonetics of the PIE expression itself, $*h_1\bar{o}\hat{k}\acute{e}\mu\text{-}es\ h_1\acute{e}\hat{k}\mu\text{-}\bar{o}s$. Although the phrase ὠκέες ἵπποι is sufficiently widespread to justify the assumption of a purely synchronically determined phonetic pattern, the fact that, prior to the recent loss of the labiovelar, the phrase had itself contained two closely positioned velar sounds raises a tantalizing prospect: that the strength of the association of velar sounds with this expression was conditioned by the expression's earlier alliterative character, which manifested a continuity of influence. If this is true, the phonetic quality of the phrase is not as far removed from its earlier linguistic phases as it initially appears. For although the expression itself does not reflect its earlier character well, the broader phonetic network in which it operates does. This would represent a continuity of phonetic treatment dating to the period when this phrase took part in the freer and more dynamic mechanics of oral composition, existing alongside the novel phonetic attractions arising after its later prominence in a consistent position. Early Greek verse does not, of course, exhibit euphonic patterning as prominently as some other IE poetries, and certainly not as prominently as some early Germanic verse or even Vedic. It is, however, reasonable to expect to see some examples of it nevertheless, perhaps especially in and around its oldest expressions, as I believe occurs here. A recognition of this may ultimately be key to seeing the relationship of these expressions to several other, less obviously related formulas.

The Formulaic Significance of Hades κλυτόπωλος

An application of the foregoing formulaic analysis to an unusual epithet of Hades will showcase just how analytically far-reaching an appreciation of euphonetic patterning can be. The adjective κλυτόπωλος ("of famous foals") appears five times in early Greek poetry, thrice in the *Iliad* as an epithet of Hades, once in the fragmentary Hesiodic *Catalogue* in reference to Ion, and later in a Pindaric fragment, where it refers to Poseidon.[35] The application of the term to Poseidon, the god of horses, is no surprise, and Ion, although not a uniquely famous horseman, is a Greek hero for whom excellence in horsemanship in expected. It is the application of the term to Hades that has confused scholars for quite some time, but I think that the emphasis on its mythological connection to Hades in the *Iliad* has precluded research into its function in oral verse. The origin of κλυτόπωλος is linked to most of the formulas outlined above, formulas that all convey the idea of "good horses." Recognizing the position of κλυτόπωλος within this formulaic network helps us to chart the diachronic evolution of this network as a whole.

The formulas described above contain an unvoiced velar in the word preceding ἵπποι, and thus contribute to an overall sense of phonetic similarity among these expressions, at the level of a basic *k...p* consonantal sequence. The semantic similarity is even easier to spot, as these particular expressions function quasi-synonymously, each having the core semantic value of 'good horses'.[36] The particularities of κλυτόπωλος will be discussed momentarily, but within this broad group most describe the horses' quality by focusing on their speed, either directly, such as ὠκέες ἵπποι and ταχέ' ἵππω, or through metonymy, such as χαλκόποδ' ἵππω and μώνυχες ἵπποι. καλλίτριχες ἵπποι and χρυσάμπυκες ἵπποι describe the horses' quality through their beauty. Rarely are these differences particularly narratologically significant. Despite the particular honorific attributes highlighted by any one expression, they all fundamentally indicate 'good horses.'

The consistency of the semantic, phonetic, and metrical quality exhibited by these expressions is striking and should not be dismissed as sheer coincidence. I suggest, in fact, that these formulas constitute an especially rich

---

[35] There are also examples of the term from later literature, but I have omitted them from this discussion because their late date removes them from the world of oral poetry. Triphiodorus uses it to describe the Achaeans, Ἅλωσις Ἰλίου, 92; Maximus Astrologus uses it to describe Selene, Περὶ Καταρχῶν, 5.75, 6.151, 6.261. It also appears once in the *Papyri Magicae Graecae* to describe Helios, Preisendanz 2.89.

[36] On the commonality of speed as a basic approbative value of horses in IE cultures see Matasovic 1996:73–4.

example of a genetically related family of formulas, similar to those studied by Nagler.[37] In such a family new expressions or formulas can be generated as something like varied allomorphic realizations of a stable underlying nexus of metrical, semantic, and phonetic characteristics. In the process of oral performance phonetically similar expressions may cluster around a unique theme, especially in common metrical positions. In this case that would mean that as a poet reached line end, the position where each of these formulas is most common, if the poet planned to express the idea of 'good horses,' a variety of different formulas may have been employed, either by generation or recollection, with the aid of a persistent underlying phonetic structure.[38]

κλυτόπωλος, differs from these expressions because it is not an adjective-noun sequence but instead a singular *bahuvrīhi*-type compound adjective, i.e. it identifies a possessor of good horses rather than the horses themselves. It nevertheless exists in the same basic semantic sphere as an expression that conveys the semantic notion of 'good horses'.[39] It also resembles these formulas at the phonetic level. In this case πῶλος (foal) appears rather than ἵππος, and κλυτός (famous) appears rather than one of the various adjectives already described, but a similar structure, anchored by corresponding *k...p* sounds is still evident. Finally, in hexametric verse this word occurs only at line end, the most frequent position for the other 'good horses' expressions. κλυτόπωλος then resembles the other members of this family at the semantic level, at the phonetic level, and at the metrical level, so satisfies the criteria for inclusion in this network. If, in the course of a performance, a poet reached line end and wished to express the core semantic idea of 'good horses' in a way that describes an individual who has good horses, rather than the good horses themselves, he could have generated or employed this expression by drawing on the same phonetic structure on which his stock of 'good horses' formulas was built.

It should be noted that the word's appearance in the Hesiodic *Catalogue* perfectly reflects its treatment in Homer, occurring in the same position as in the Homeric texts:

ἥ οι Ἀ]χαιὸν ἐγ ἐγ[είνατ' Ἰάονά τε κλυ]τόπωλ[ο]ν
μιχθ]εῖσ' ἐγ [φιλότητι καὶ εὐε]ιδέα Διομήδην

---

[37] Nagler 1967:269–291.

[38] Such associations may also explain the unusual consistency of the *nu* that so often precedes the accusative formulas discussed above.

[39] cf. Apion's definition: 'ἵππους ἀγαθοὺς <ἔχων>', Γλῶσσαι (*Sammlung griechischer und lateinischer Grammatiker*) 3, fr. 51.1.

who bore to him Akhaios, and Ion of famous foals, and glorious Diomedes, having mingled in love

Solmsen frag. 10a23–24

The only other early usage occurs in Pindar, and is the only one that deviates from this pattern:

Ζηνὸς υἱοὶ καὶ κλυτοπώλου Ποσειδάωνος

the sons of Zeus and Poseidon of famous foals

Maehler frag. 243.2

This is, however, a metrical outlier, occurring in non-hexametric verse, and Pindaric poetry was presumably composed with the aid of writing, so this particular example does not need to have an origin in oral verse mechanics. It is not uncommon, however, for Pindar's compositions to employ ancient phraseologies or to display vestiges of older technique.[40] In any case the Pindaric usage does nothing to obscure the character of this term or related terms in earlier verse.[41]

To gain an understanding of the full significance of this term's relationship to the horse formulas discussed above, a look at other uses of the word πῶλος, "foal," in the epics is instructive. The word is used relatively seldom, at least in comparison to ἵπποι, "horses," and it usually occurs in compounds. The very few examples of πῶλος occurring in uncompounded form appear in the immediate vicinity of the word ἵππος and may be employed there to avoid repetition. In its more common compound forms it usually occurs at verse end, often in the formula Δαναῶν ταχυπώλων, "of the Danaans of swift foals." This appears ten times in the epics, and it too exhibits the same phonetic character as the broader family under discussion. πῶλος also appears twice in the name Ἐχέπωλος, "the

---

[40] Pindar may, in fact, showcase other members of this family not attested in Homer. λεύκιπποι, and λευκόπωλοι, the bright horses, for example, are both absent from Homer but display the same underlying phonetic structure as the Homeric 'good horses' formulas.

[41] One more term, πλήξιππος ("lasher of horses") may also be added to the list of related expressions in Homer, since it features the same phonetic structure and in three of its four appearance in the *Iliad* it appears at verse end (II 104, IV 327, XI 93). Admittedly, it does not agree with the others semantically in quite as neat a fashion, but it does indicate one's status as horseman and so could function in the same broad nexus of expressions. Moreover, the word is slightly unusual because compounds that feature ἵππος as their final element are fairly rare, as is generally the case of compounds in which a verbal element precedes a nominal, i.e. the "pickpocket" compounds. The system proposed here may provide some justification for this unusual form.

possessor of foals," which also occurs at line end and also demonstrates the same phonetic character.

Πρῶτος δ' Ἀντίλοχος Τρώων ἕλεν ἄνδρα κορυστὴν
ἐσθλὸν ἐνὶ προμάχοισι Θαλυσιάδην Ἐχέπωλον·

Antilokhos first slew one of the helmeted Trojans among the fore-fighters, noble Ekhepolos, son of Thalusios.

Iliad IV 457–458

Ἴλιον εἰς εὔπωλον, "toward Ilium of the good foals," is the only common usage not accounted for by these phonetic and metrical constraints.

The recognition of πῶλος within this network is especially exciting because it helps us to chart the development of the network with unusual precision by allowing us to identify an early and a late phase. *$h_1\bar{o}k\acute{e}\mu$-es $h_1\acute{e}k\mu$-ōs surely proliferated in Greek before the period documented in our texts and, most importantly, before the significant phonetic developments discussed above, specifically, the conversion of Greek labiovelars, the $k\mu$ sounds, to *p* in many contexts, including when they were followed by an *o* as happened here.[42] Again, in the period just before that which our texts document, this formula was certainly in use, but did not sound like ὠκέες ἵπποι, but instead like ὠκέϝες ἵκϝοι, with two unvoiced velar sounds. The organizing phonetic structure then was not, in fact, the *k...p* sequence that the Homeric formula family documents. The original underlying phonetic structure seems instead to have been an alliterative *k...k*.

This presents a problem, however, for the two halves of this formula family, the expressions anchored to a final ἵππος unit and those anchored to a final πῶλος unit, like κλυτόπωλος. The etymology of πῶλος is still the subject of speculation, but it must descend from something like *polH-. Thieme has suggested that this comes from the verbal root *$k\mu el$-,[43] meaning "to roam," but its perfect cognition with such words as German *Fohlen* and Gothic *fula*, and even English "foal" makes that impossible. The unvoiced labiovelar $k\mu$ sound could indeed become a labial *p* in Greek but would not have become a fricative *f* in the Germanic languages. A *p*, as in *polH-, would yield precisely what we see in the Greek and the Germanic cognates.[44] This means that πῶλος always began with a

---

[42] I must repeat here that the word ἵππος may never have contained an actual labio-velar, but instead a velar followed by a labial, but that this difference should be insignificant for this analysis. See note 14.

[43] Thieme 1968:143–148.

[44] There are other cognates that support this as well. See Beekes 2013:1266 and Frisk 1970:2.634.

p sound and that the underlying phonetic structure for the πῶλος formulas was always *k...p*, rather than the *k...k* of the ἵππος formulas.

The best explanation for the relationship of these two groups must lie in a diachronic evolution of the phonetic schema of which all these formulas are a realization. This is an evolution that would have occurred in tandem with the changing phonetic character of the Greek language. The ἵππος formulas, or more historically, the ἵκϝος formulas, must represent an earlier phase in the generation of "good horses" expressions. In early oral composition "good horses" expressions must have employed an alliterative *k...k* pattern, perhaps rooted in the *figura etymologica* of the "swift swifties" phenomenon. As the phonetic evolution of the Greek language altered the ἵκϝος formulas to ἵππος formulas, the schema upon which all of these expressions were founded altered as well, developing from a *k...k* structure to a *k...p*. After phonetic change resulted in this *k...p* sequence this new scheme became generative itself and thenceforth formulas could be added to the network with a base in ἵππος or πῶλος. This does not mean, of course, that each unique ἵππος formula must antedate each unique πῶλος formula, but instead that the general practice of generating and employing ἵππος formulas must have a start date anterior to the start date of the incorporation of πῶλος formulas.

The Iliadic treatment of κλυτόπωλος then provides excellent evidence for understanding the development and deployment of horse formulas generally in Greek oral poetry. But what of its application to Hades? Although few scholars have looked into this term very deeply, those who have have focused entirely on explaining why Hades would be known as a possessor of famous foals in the first place. Horses do not after all feature very frequently in his mythology. Although my own argument here has not yet dealt with this issue, it has been implicit throughout my reasoning that there was indeed some special significance in the application of the term to Hades. My argument in fact assumes that the Greek oral poets deployed this term for one who possesses good horses on the model of "good horses" formulas precisely because there was an immediate utility to such a term in their performances, and this argument must not conclude, I think, without attempting to identify what that was.

The first step in this process should be an examination of the occurrences of the term themselves:

Sarpedon speaking to Tlepolemus:

σοὶ δ' ἐγὼ ἐνθάδε φημὶ φόνον καὶ κῆρα μέλαιναν
ἐξ ἐμέθεν τεύξεσθαι, ἐμῷ δ' ὑπὸ δουρὶ δαμέντα
εὖχος ἐμοὶ δώσειν, ψυχὴν δ' Ἄϊδι <u>κλυτοπώλῳ</u>.

I declare that slaughter and dark death will be fashioned for you, by my hands and that you, conquered by my spear, will give glory to me and your soul <u>to Hades of famous foals</u>.

Iliad V 652–654

Odysseus speaking to Socus:

σοὶ δ' ἐγὼ ἐνθάδε φημὶ φόνον καὶ κῆρα μέλαιναν
ἤματι τῷδ' ἔσσεσθαι, ἐμῷ δ' ὑπὸ δουρὶ δαμέντα
εὖχος ἐμοὶ δώσειν, ψυχὴν δ' <u>Ἄϊδι κλυτοπώλῳ</u>.

I declare that there will be slaughter and dark death for you today, and that you, conquered by my spear, will give glory to me and your soul <u>to Hades of famous foals</u>.

Iliad XI 443–445

Meriones speaking to Aeneas:

εἰ καὶ ἐγώ σε βάλοιμι τυχὼν μέσον ὀξέϊ χαλκῷ,
αἶψά κε καὶ κρατερός περ ἐὼν καὶ χερσὶ πεποιθὼς
εὖχος ἐμοὶ δοίης, ψυχὴν δ' <u>Ἄϊδι κλυτοπώλῳ</u>.

If I should hurl [my spear] at you, and strike your middle with my sharp bronze, although you are strong and trust your hands, you would quickly give glory to me and your soul <u>to Hades of famous foals</u>.

Iliad XVI 623–625

The first thing that one notices is that Ἄϊδι κλυτοπώλῳ is not the only common element among these passages, but that these lines echo each other generally, as if a traditional threat has been adapted three times. This looks then like an element of a type-scene, a narratological unit, larger than any single formula, in which elements tend to cluster in a given type of scene. One may still ask, however, why it is κλυτόπωλος that we find embedded in these important lines rather than one of Hades' other epithets. There are five such epithets in the Homeric poems: ἴφθιμος ("mighty"), ἀδάμαστος ("unconquerable"), πελώριος ("monstrous" or "huge"), ἀμείλιχος ("implacable"), and πυλάρτης ("gate fastener"). It is important that these are not all strictly interchangeable, however. Each one is metrically unique and served its own function in the process of composition in performance.[45] These six epithets in fact form their

---

[45] ἴφθιμος is particularly interesting because it is only used of Hades himself in the *Odyssey*, while in the *Iliad* it occurs in proximity to Hades but modifies the souls and the heads of the men who die and are sent to him (I 3; XI 55).

own formulaic network, one that overlaps with the network under examination here, and in which κλυτόπωλος plays an important role.

The term κλυτόπωλος is unlikely to have been chosen from this network for metrical reasons alone, and we should still look to these lines for nonmetrical motivations. Since it is not this epithet alone that repeats but the threat's language generally, the question that we must ask is not just why Hades would have famous foals but why his possession of them would be significant in this particular type of scene, in which this language was apparently resonant enough to become traditional. The answer here must be related to the passages' striking similarity of context: each occurrence is part of a threat that sudden death will soon befall the target of the speaker's aggression. What, then, does the epithet κλυτόπωλος have to do with such sudden death? It is with this question in mind that we should turn our attention to the two scholars who have studied this word in depth, Paul Thieme, mentioned earlier, and Martin P. Nilsson.[46] Although neither approached the word in quite this light, each offers very useful suggestions about the application of κλυτόπωλος to Hades.

Thieme's explanation has roots in the IE underworld and the etymology of the word "Hades" itself, which is complicated. He suggests that the word is comprised of the prefix *sm̥*- 'with' and the verbal root **ueid*- 'to see'. Thieme's etymology would roughly mean 'seeing together', and would have a perfect cognate in the particularly loaded Sanskrit term *saṃvedanam*, referring to the act of reuniting with one's forefathers in the afterlife.[47] He suggests that the limited information that we have about the early IE afterlife suggests that this realm was imagined, at least in part, as a meadowland, and therefore may have contained horses.[48] If Thieme is correct, then these lines and the word κλυτόπωλος within

---

[46] I omit here the argument of Verrall (1898) that the term had nothing to do with horses at all but rather with "ranging" and "haunting," as if connected to πωλέομαι. Pindar's application of the word to Poseidon, the horse god, makes his idea difficult to accept.

[47] Puhvel also points out (1987:109) that the Vedic Yama is the *saṃgámanam jánānām*, "ingatherer of the people." The more traditional etymology traces the word to **ṇu̯id*- 'unseen', which not only corresponds with the basic notion that death is unforeseeable, but is particularly apt given Hades' possession of a cap that imbued its wearer with invisibility (cf. Apollodorus *Bibliotheca* I 2.1 and *The Shield* 226–227; Pherekydes 3 F 11). See Frisk 1970:1.33.

[48] Although beyond the scope of this argument, there are some other pieces of Indic evidence that could be added to bolster the connection between horses and the ruler of the dead. The name of the Indo-Iranian underworld god, Yama (Sanskrit)/Yima (Avestan) does appear to have something to do with reining, and the Sanskrit noun *yama* when it does not appear as a name can indicate a rein. Yama is also said to have had particularly good horses, but that is true of the subjects of too many Vedic hymns to be useful: e.g. *hiraṇyakaśyānsudhurān hiraṇākṣānayaśśaphān aśvānanaśyato*, "horses with golden girdles, good under the yoke, golden eyed, and iron hoofed, immortal" (*Taittirīya Āraṇyaka* 6.5.2.5–6). For other similarities between the Greek and Indic afterworld see Puhvel 1987:139. On the Yama analogues in Greek mythology more generally see Ehni 1890:196–209.

them would serve to call to mind the place to which the threatened man may soon be going. This works very well here, because the epithet would not be incidental but specially suited to this particularly narratological circumstance, making sense of its unique occurrence in minatory exchange. Although this could be a sufficient explanation for the expression, it does require that the term be a fossilization, because the belief that there were horses in the underworld is not attested in archaic Greece. This expression would need to have been preserved by poetic habit after its original significance had been forgotten. Although this is possible, I think it is useful to explore the possibility that this phrase had synchronic significance as well, to ask if it meant something special to the archaic poet and audience, admitting that such a meaning does not need to be the meaning of its origin. This is, I think, an especially important line of inquiry given scholarly debate about Thieme's etymology.[49]

For this I turn to Nilsson, whose explanation is followed by most scholars. He suggests that the term adheres because of Hades' use of horses in the abduction of Persephone.[50] This theory holds that Hades did not always await the arrival of new souls to the underworld, but instead came on occasion to the realm of the living to collect them. This particular element of Hades' behavior would be typified in the abduction of Persephone. Hades' horses would feature in this epithet because they are the means by which he hunts down his victims; they function metonymically, like the Grim Reaper's sickle. Contrary to Nilsson's suggestion, however, I do not believe that there is good evidence showing that Hades was often imagined carrying souls to the underworld via his chariot,[51] but instead Persephone seems to be the only figure about whom this is said to have happened. I suggest that this is the best starting point for this analysis. For although horses are not a frequent feature of Hades' mythology, his abduction of Persephone by chariot was an exceedingly important and prolific story. Reference to Hades' horses then would not remind the archaic audience of the underworld generally but of the sudden and violent abduction of Persephone specifically. The import of this minatory usage may, in fact, be that the victim is about to go to the underworld suddenly, just as Persephone did. The epithet need be neither incidental nor vestigial here but may have worked specifically to enhance the resonance of the language of the associated threat. Such a reading is, of course, impossible to verify conclusively but seems to me to provide the

---

[49] On objections to Thieme's etymology see Beekes 2013:34.

[50] Nilsson 1941:I 425.

[51] The only evidence that could support this, that I know of, comes from epitaphs that occasionally describe Hades snatching (ἁρπάζω) the dead: e.g. *Inscriptiones Graecae* II² 12629, *Supplementum Epigraphicum Graecum* 25.298. Even then, however, this seems usually to indicate the death of a young woman and may then still be a reference to the Persephone myth.

most promising hypothesis since it allows room for diachronic evolution of the phrase while still pointing the way to a synchronic utility that aided in the epithet's survival.

Although the epithet κλυτόπωλος appears only three times in the *Iliad*, its occurrence offers us special insights concerning the prehistory of Homeric horse formulas. It also highlights the profound role that the phrase ὠκέες ἵπποι has in the history of Greek epic, as well as the place that it should have in our analysis of Homeric equine poetics. For not only do the metrical deployment and phonetic structure of κλυτόπωλος reflect common metrical and phonetic characteristics among the formulas related to ὠκέες ἵπποι, but the linguistic history of the epithet's final element, πῶλος, allows us a glimpse of diachronic evolution within Homeric horse formulas generally. Its *p* sound has always been a *p* sound, while the *p* sound of formulas anchored by ἵππος was originally a *k* sound, and this allows us to identify two groups within this family of formulas, those that were always built on a *k...p* structure, like κλυτόπωλος, and those whose historic *k...p* structure reflects a prehistoric *k...k* structure, like ὠκέες ἵπποι. Given the ancient poetic qualities of the *k...k* formulas and the extreme age of their most prominent representative, ὠκέες ἵπποι, it must be the case that the production of ἵππος formulas predates the production of πῶλος formulas. κλυτόπωλος then proves a precious window into the deep history of these oral formulas as well as the practices of the poets who employed them. Although linguistic changes in a language must sometimes render poetic expressions obsolete, κλυτόπωλος provides beautiful evidence of how oral formulas survive those changes, and how traditional poetic expressions sometimes persist and even multiply, yielding new forms and new meanings over the millennia.

2

Horses, Heroes, and Sacrifice

THE PROMINENT POSITION OF THE FORMULA ὠκέες ἵπποι and related expressions attests the special role played in Greek epic by horses and the physical abilities that distinguish them. The similarity of formulas in both Indian and Iranian oral poetries makes it clear that the phrase indicates a common poetic inheritance. It is a sensible assumption that a formula about horses that is important enough to be maintained in all three cultures would accompany other poetic and cultural treatments of horses that were also commonly inherited. In fact, the similarities in the treatment of horses found in the descendant traditions do extend beyond vocabulary.

They are especially manifest in the relationship between horses and heroes, which appears to be rooted in a common predisposition toward the anthropomorphizing of horses and the concomitant hippomorphizing of humans.[1] Perhaps this tendency is to be expected given the nature of the genres in which our evidence is found, yet the particularities of this phenomenon are sufficiently unique that a common inheritance may reasonably be sought. Additionally, research into a prominent horse sacrifice ritual in the parent culture reveals several insights into the nature of this common inheritance, namely that a ritualistic shift in identity between horse and human was central to the event. A survey of our Greek, Sanskrit, and other IE evidence will demonstrate the case for common inheritance and provide a vantage point from which surprising aspects of the Greek treatment of horses become comprehensible. I will first review some idiosyncrasies of the relationship between horses and heroes in

---

[1] Hippomorphism in IE texts is also discussed by Puhvel (1987:274). I use the term slightly more loosely, in discussion not only of literal, physical hippomorphism but of metaphorical hippomorphism as well, i.e. of poetic and ritualistic treatments of human shape or physicality as fundamentally like that of a horse. Similarly, I talk of anthropomorphism in cases wherein horses are treated in the same way, vis-à-vis humans.

Greek epic, in order to isolate it as a phenomenon worthy of this sort of analysis. Then I will evaluate the evidence for the PIE horse sacrifice and discuss its relevance to the current issue, ultimately suggesting that a unique model for understanding the relationship between horses and humans informed that ritual and that that model, if not the ritual itself, exerted lengthy influence over Greece.

Heroes as Horses and Horses as Heroes

Before proceeding to cross-cultural and historical parallels, then, I will discuss some special details of horse/hero comparisons that are generally found in Greek epic. The fact that there is a close connection between the two is not surprising, but the depth and nature of this link is truly unique and not, I think, common outside of the IE world. First, the similarity between horses and heroes begins at the level of ontology.[2] Not only are both essential figures of martial excellence, but horses are seemingly unique in the animal world for sharing with humans, especially heroic humans, the capacity for divine lineage and semi-divine identity. Several Greek gods have immortal horses that are known by name, such as those of Ares, Helios, and the Dioskouroi.[3] Yet immortal horses that live among mortals are more important for the current discussion, and there are several. For example, Pausanias describes the very powerful horse, Areion, owned by Herakles and then by Adrastus, which was born from the coupling of Poseidon and Demeter when both gods had assumed the form of horses:[4]

> πλανωμένη γὰρ τῇ Δήμητρι, ἡνίκα τὴν παῖδα ἐζήτει, λέγουσιν ἕπεσθαί
> οἱ τὸν Ποσειδῶνα ἐπιθυμοῦντα αὐτῇ μιχθῆναι, καὶ τὴν μὲν ἐς ἵππον
> μεταβαλοῦσαν ὁμοῦ ταῖς ἵπποις νέμεσθαι ταῖς Ὀγκίου, Ποσειδῶν δὲ
> συνίησεν ἀπατώμενος καὶ συγγίνεται τῇ Δήμητρι ἄρσενι ἵππῳ καὶ αὐτὸς
> εἰκασθείς...τὴν δὲ Δήμητρα τεκεῖν φασιν ἐκ τοῦ Ποσειδῶνος θυγατέρα,
> ἧς τὸ ὄνομα ἐς ἀτελέστους λέγειν οὐ νομίζουσι, καὶ ἵππον τὸν Ἀρείονα·

> They say that while Demeter was searching for her daughter, Poseidon followed her, desiring to couple with her, and that she, having changed

---

2 The treatment of horse-taming as a measure of one's heroic valor is also common in Greek epic, but I will not look at that topic extensively in this work. For a survey of the evidence, however, see Macurdy 1923.

3 Quintus Smyrnaeus VIII 242; Ovid *Metamorphoses* II 153–154; Stesichorus frag. 178.

4 See also Apollodorus III 77 and Hesiod *Shield* 120. Demeter and Poseidon are not the only deities to have produced a child while in horse form. Cronos is said to have mated with Phillyra while in horse-form as well. The union is part of one of the competing genealogies of the centaur Chiron, to be discussed in the appendix.

into a horse, grazed among the mares of Onkios. Poseidon, however, realizing that he had been tricked, mated with Demeter, having changed his own form to that of a stallion. They say that Demeter bore a daughter by Poseidon, whose name they believe should not be told to the uninitiated, and a horse named Areion.

Pausanias VIII 25.5–7

This horse is also mentioned in the *Iliad* in connection with other divine horses:

οὐκ ἔσθ' ὅς κέ σ' ἕλῃσι μετάλμενος οὐδὲ παρέλθῃ,
οὐδ' εἴ κεν μετόπισθεν Ἀρίονα δῖον ἐλαύνοι
Ἀδρήστου ταχὺν ἵππον, ὃς ἐκ θεόφιν γένος ἦεν,
ἢ τοὺς Λαομέδοντος, οἳ ἐνθάδε γ' ἔτραφεν ἐσθλοί.

There is no one who could catch you with a burst of speed or pass you by, not even if he were driving behind you the lordly Areion, the swift horse of Adrastus, who was born of the gods, or the horses of Laomedon, the noble horses raised here.

Iliad XXIII 345–348

The local Trojan horses mentioned here are the divine horses given to Laomedon by Zeus as recompense for the abduction of Ganymede. The horses of Aeneas, which feature so prominently in the *Iliad* due to their abduction by Diomedes and subsequent victory in the chariot race at the funeral games of Patroclus, are descendants of these horses.[5] In book XX, Aeneas recalls the story of the three thousand mares of Erichthonius, which mated with Boreas, the god of the North Wind, and produced twelve colts that could run over the top of the sea.[6]

τοῦ τρισχίλιαι ἵπποι ἕλος κάτα βουκολέοντο
θήλειαι, πώλοισιν ἀγαλλόμεναι ἀταλῇσι.
τάων καὶ Βορέης ἠράσσατο βοσκομενάων,
ἵππῳ δ' εἰσάμενος παρελέξατο κυανοχαίτῃ·
αἳ δ' ὑποκυσάμεναι ἔτεκον δυοκαίδεκα πώλους.
αἳ δ' ὅτε μὲν σκιρτῷεν ἐπὶ ζείδωρον ἄρουραν,
ἄκρον ἐπ' ἀνθερίκων καρπὸν θέον οὐδὲ κατέκλων·
ἀλλ' ὅτε δὴ σκιρτῷεν ἐπ' εὐρέα νῶτα θαλάσσης,
ἄκρον ἐπὶ ῥηγμῖνος ἁλὸς πολιοῖο θέεσκον.

---

[5] *Iliad* V 263–269.
[6] The phenomenon of animals impregnated by the wind is documented in other Greco-Roman sources as well. For extensive treatment see Zirkle 1936.

His three thousand horses grazed along the marsh-land, mares
delighting in their tender foals. And Boreas became enamored of them
while they pastured and, assuming the form of a dark-maned stallion,
he mated with them. They conceived and bore twelve colts, which,
when they bounded over the fruitful land, raced over the topmost ears
of corn without breaking them, and, when they bounded over the wide
back of the sea, they raced over the tops of the waves of the hoary sea.

Iliad XX 221–229

Furthermore, part of what makes Achilles special on the battlefield is that
he has three horses attached to his chariot—unlike most fighters, who have
only two—and that two of his are immortal. At the time of the events of the
Iliad he has only recently added the mortal horse, Pedasos, while his permanent
team of Xanthos and Balios are the immortal offspring of the Harpy Podarge, an
especially appropriate name for the progenitor of famous steeds. Horses, then,
share with humans, especially heroic humans, an ontological position unique
among living things: they may descend from the gods and maintain some divine
capacity derived from them. In the same way that heroes are marked out from
the rest of humanity by their divine lineages, so then are their horses. Like the
demigods they are descended from immortals, equine or godly, and in some
cases capable of inheriting from them immortality themselves, as Herakles did
from Zeus and his horse Areion did from Poseidon and Demeter.

Other divine animals do exist in the form of the signature animals of the
gods, such as the owl of Athena. Yet this does not mean that these animals are
immortal, at least not that they are immortal in the same way that gods and
divine horses can be, because these animals are not usually given individual
identities, names, or genealogies. They are also depicted only as the companions
and emblems of the gods, and not as their descendants, a status which seems
reserved for humans and horses alone. They are essentially iconographic and
rarely constitute actors on the mythical stage.[7] The character of divine horses
seems to be fundamentally different from that of other animals, and to draw
them ontologically closer to the heroes whom they accompany than to other
animals.

The potential of horses to share with heroes characteristics of essential
identity extends to a similarity in poetic treatment as well. Horses within the
Iliad are regarded as heroes by the human characters of the poem as well as by

---

[7] Rare exceptions exist, such as the crow of Apollo who informed him of the love affair of Coronis.
This, however, seems quite different from the role of divine horses, who exist as a broader class,
yet are more individualized and have more developed mythologies.

its narrator, and occasionally treated like their owners themselves. For example in book VIII Hector urges his four horses to battle,[8] calling them by name and saying:

Ξάνθέ τε καὶ σὺ Πόδαργε καὶ Αἴθων Λάμπέ τε δῖε
νῦν μοι τὴν κομιδὴν ἀποτίνετον, ἣν μάλα πολλὴν
Ἀνδρομάχη θυγάτηρ μεγαλήτορος Ἠετίωνος
ὑμῖν πὰρ προτέροισι μελίφρονα πυρὸν ἔθηκεν
οἶνόν τ' ἐγκεράσασα πιεῖν, ὅτε θυμὸς ἀνώγοι,
ἢ ἐμοί, ὅς πέρ οἱ θαλερὸς πόσις εὔχομαι εἶναι.

Xanthos, and you, Podargos, and Aithon and noble Lampos, now pay back the provision of honey-hearted wheat, that Andromache, the daughter of great-hearted Eëtion gave to you in great quantity, and wine that she mixed for you to drink whenever your heart bade, which she gave to you even before me, I who am proud to be her husband.[9]

Iliad VIII 185–190

The fact that these horses drink wine at all distinguishes them from other animals since wine is a mark of human civilization. This act essentially isolates a species boundary, a boundary that positions horses as closer to humans than to other animals. The use of the phrase ὅτε θυμὸς ἀνώγοι is also striking and is translated here as "whenever your heart bade," and is assumed to refer to the horses. It could, however, be argued that this clause refers to Andromache's desire rather than to the horses', that it should be translated as "whenever her heart bade." Yet the formula πιέειν ὅτε θυμὸς ἀνώγοι appears elsewhere twice in the Homeric corpus and in each case πιέειν complements ἀνώγοι,[10] so the heart of the figure by whom the wine is to be drunk is the subject of the verb ἀνώγοι. If that relationship holds true in this usage then the horses here display a degree of agency otherwise reserved for humans. It may be pointed out that this entire line was athetized by the Alexandrian editors, signaling their discom-

---

[8] Achilles and Hector are the only Homeric heroes with more than two horses attached to their chariots. It is noteworthy that the unique position of these heroes among their peoples and their unique relationship to each other, which comprises the narratological climax of the work, the battle between Achilles and Hector, is reflected by their abundance of horses. On the number of horses possessed by heroes both in the *Iliad* and elsewhere, see Delebecque 1951:143–144.

[9] The participle ἐγκεράσασα could imply that she mixed the wine in a bowl or that she mixed it in with the food. The former makes better sense with the infinitive πιεῖν while the latter has seemed more reasonable to most readers; see Kirk 1990:313. In either case, that fact that the horses consume wine is remarkable and, I think, heroic.

[10] *Iliad* IV 263, *Odyssey* viii 70. This formula also appears modified in *Odyssey* xvi 141, πίνε καὶ ἦσθ', ὅτε θυμὸς ἐνὶ στήθεσσιν ἀνώγοι, "He drank and he ate whenever the heart in his chest bade."

fort with the depiction of the horses drinking wine at all. Be that as it may, the image did appear in the ancient tradition, and did so because the offering of wine to heroes was a regular feature of Greek oral song and these horses are here treated as heroes, rather than as ordinary animals.

This attitude toward horses and heroes is also observable in the narrator of the poem himself. Near the end of the catalogue of ships he asks the goddess for special inspiration so that he may know who the very best of the warriors at Troy were:

οὗτοι ἄρ' ἡγεμόνες Δαναῶν καὶ κοίρανοι ἦσαν·
τίς τ' ἄρ τῶν ὄχ' ἄριστος ἔην σύ μοι ἔννεπε Μοῦσα
αὐτῶν ἠδ' ἵππων, οἳ ἅμ' Ἀτρεΐδησιν ἕποντο.

These were the leaders and commanders of the Danaans. But tell me, o Muse, who was the very best of the men and of the horses that followed with the sons of Atreus.

Iliad II 760–762

Her inspired answer is:

ἵπποι μὲν μέγ' ἄρισται ἔσαν Φηρητιάδαο,
τὰς Εὔμηλος ἔλαυνε ποδώκεας ὄρνιθας ὣς

...

ἀνδρῶν αὖ μέγ' ἄριστος ἔην Τελαμώνιος Αἴας
ὄφρ Ἀχιλεὺς μήνιεν· ὃ γὰρ πολὺ φέρτατος ἦεν,
ἵπποι θ', οἳ φορέεσκον ἀμύμονα Πηλεΐωνα.

The best horses were the mares of the son of Pheres, the ones that Eumelus drove, swift like birds...And by far the best of men was Telemonian Ajax, so long, that is, as Achilles was raging. For he was indeed the most powerful, as were his horses, those who bore the incomparable son of Peleus.

Iliad II 763–764; 768–770

The narrator in fact also often compares heroes to horses, and even interweaves elements of the horses and their owners' identities. The epic fighters in general wear horsehair-crested helmets, giving the impression that they have a horse's mane. Horses are fitted out for battle along with warriors, who don a piece of clothing that makes them look, at least a little, like horses. Griffith expresses this very well: "The horse-hair plumes of these helmets blend valor with exuberance, horsiness with humanity." [11] The dressing of both hero and horse works to assimilate the two figures visually. Some heroes can also be specially marked out by their identification with their horses, as a quick look at Diomedes and his horses will prove. In book V, when Aeneas is talking to Pandarus about the unknown man raging on the battlefield, Pandarus replies that he knows that man to be Diomedes, in part because of his horses. He says:

Τυδείδη μιν ἔγωγε δαΐφρονι πάντα ἐΐσκω,
ἀσπίδι γιγνώσκων αὐλώπιδί τε τρυφαλείη,
ἵππους τ᾽ εἰσορόων.

I liken him in all ways to [Diomedes] the son of Tydeus, knowing him by his shield, his crested helmet, and by looking at his horses.

Iliad V 181–183

It is ironic that these horses by which Diomedes is recognized are the very horses that he will forsake for the semi-divine Trojan horses that he steals from Aeneas. Yet, the story of Diomedes in the *Iliad* is largely the story of a lesser hero stepping temporarily into the role of Achilles, and, in a sense, his heroic ascent is paralleled by his equestrian ascent. Pandarus, on the other hand, is best known for his archery and is unique among the Trojan fighters in not having any horses at all. When Aeneas asks him to assume the role of his charioteer in book V he does so because Pandarus has just explained that he has no horses of his own because he left them all in his homeland.[12] He says in line 201 ἦ τ᾽ ἂν πολὺ κέρδιον ἦεν, "it would have been much better [if I had brought horses]." It is difficult to avoid thinking that the life that he leads at Troy, tricked into breaking the truce and finally killed, pierced through the tongue by Diomedes, is somehow presaged by his unusual dearth of horses, the warrior's standard accoutrement and the very status marker in which Diomedes is excelling.

Furthermore, Diomedes upbraids the aged horseman Nestor for being out on the battlefield past his prime by criticizing his horses and by extension Nestor himself:

ὦ γέρον ἦ μάλα δή σε νέοι τείρουσι μαχηταί,
σὴ δὲ βίη λέλυται, χαλεπὸν δέ σε γῆρας ὀπάζει,
ἠπεδανὸς δέ νύ τοι θεράπων, βραδέες δέ τοι ἵπποι.

---

[11] Griffith 2006:315.
[12] See *Iliad* V 192–203.

ἀλλ' ἄγ' ἐμῶν ὀχέων ἐπιβήσεο, ὄφρα ἴδηαι
οἷοι Τρώϊοι ἵπποι

Old man, indeed the young fighters are wearing you out. Your strength
is sapped and harsh old age oppresses you. Your attendant is weak and
your horses are slow. But come, mount my chariot and see of what sort
are the horses of Troy.

Iliad VIII 102–106

Nestor's old age is mirrored in the slowness of his horses while the superiority of Diomedes is reflected in the high quality of his, despite the fact that
the horses have only recently been stolen from Aeneas. That the horses did not
originally belong to Diomedes is not an issue: his present status as a fighter
is perfectly matched by his current steeds, perhaps especially because he has
proven his superiority over Aeneas by taking those horses. Diomedes' superior stature means that the worthier horses are properly his regardless of their
provenance.

This identification of horse and hero finds its most consistent expression
in Achilles and his mixed triad of mortal and immortal horses. Achilles' own
horse-like qualities are signaled by his legendary speed as well as by his sharing
of the epithet "swift-footed" with Iliadic horses. In turn, the human-like quality
of his horses is made clear by the famous episodes in which they shed tears
at the death of Patroclus[13] and in which one of the horses, Xanthos, rebukes
Achilles for accusing the horses of allowing Patroclus' death.[14] The close identity between Achilles and his horses is reflected in their relationship to immortality. As mentioned earlier, Xanthos and Balios[15] are the immortal offspring of
a Harpy, and Pedasos, though mortal, is nevertheless swift enough to keep pace
with the immortal horses:

τῷ δὲ καὶ Αὐτομέδων ὕπαγε ζυγὸν ὠκέας ἵππους
Ξάνθον καὶ Βαλίον, τὼ ἅμα πνοιῇσι πετέσθην,
τούς ἔτεκε Ζεφύρῳ ἀνέμῳ Ἅρπυια Ποδάργη
βοσκομένη λειμῶνι παρὰ ῥόον Ὠκεανοῖο.

---

[13] *Iliad* XVII 426.
[14] *Iliad* XIX 404–417. On Xanthos as a conflation of other talking horses see Johnston 1992. Talking
horses are not, of course, entirely rare outside of the Homeric epics. They are common enough
in folk tales, such as Grimm Brothers' *Die Gänsemagd* and *Dapplegrim*, and are quite well known
in epic poetry outside of Greece. See Bowra 1961:165–169. The Ṛgvedic figure Dadhyac speaks in
hymn 1.119.9 with a horse head having replaced his own.
[15] Balios is unusual among epic horses in not having an etymologically transparent name. For a
discussion of the possible Illyrian etymology see Athanassakis 2002.

ἐν δὲ παρηορίῃσιν ἀμύμονα Πήδασον ἵει,
τόν ῥά ποτ' Ἠετίωνος ἑλὼν πόλιν ἤγαγ' Ἀχιλλεύς,
ὃς καὶ θνητὸς ἐὼν ἔπεθ' ἵπποις ἀθανάτοισι.

And Automedon yoked the swift horses, Xanthos and Balios, those that flew with the wind, which the Harpy Podarge bore to the West Wind while grazing in a meadow beside the stream of Okeanos.[16] In the side traces he sent faultless Pedasos, whom Achilles had once driven after sacking the city of Eëtion.[17] Although mortal he followed along with the immortal horses.

Iliad XVI 148–154

The mixture of mortal and immortal components in his chariot team reflects the genealogy of Achilles himself, the son of a goddess, Thetis, and a human, Peleus.[18] We hear twice in the *Iliad*, once from Odysseus and once from Apollo, that no one but Achilles can drive his horses properly and that this is due to a similarity in their makeup. One of these instances occurs in book X, when Dolon confesses to Odysseus that he spied on the Trojan camp because Hector had promised him the horses of Achilles in return. Odysseus replies:

ἦ ῥά νύ τοι μεγάλων δώρων ἐπεμαίετο θυμός·
ἵππων Αἰακίδαο δαΐφρονος· οἳ δ' ἀλεγεινοὶ
ἀνδράσι γε θνητοῖσι δαμήμεναι ἠδ' ὀχέεσθαι
ἄλλῳ γ' ἢ Ἀχιλῆϊ, τὸν ἀθανάτη τέκε μήτηρ.

Indeed your heart was set on great gifts, the horses of the battle-minded son of Aeacus, but they are hard for mortal men to tame and drive, for any man but Achilles, whom an immortal mother bore.

Iliad X 401–404

---

[16] The Harpies are themselves associated with the wind and, at times, are almost an expression of it: *Odyssey* xx 66–77. One of the Harpies, Ἀελλώ, even takes her name from the word for storm-wind, ἄελλα; see *Theogony* 267.

[17] It will be noticed that Andromache and Pedasos both come from the same city, Thebe, which was controlled by Andromache's father, Eëtion. The city was sacked by Achilles and his Myrmidons before the war at Troy. While Achilles took the horse from the city for himself, Andromache escaped, the sole survivor in her family, and fled to Troy, where she married Hector. In epic, women and horses are both treated, in some sense, as moveable property.

[18] Although the horse genealogy considered here is by far the most common reflected in our sources, an account of Xanthos and Balios in Diodorus Siculus VI 3 claims that they were once Titans who were so ashamed of their relation to the other Titans that they asked Zeus to alter their shape.

The team is unmanageable to others because it is partly divine but can be mastered by Achilles, who is also partly divine, the son of the goddess Thetis. Yet it is singularly important that neither Achilles nor his chariot team is entirely divine, because the narratological focus is frequently not on the two immortal horses but on the mortal one, Pedasos, just as the narratological focus of the epic is on Achilles' mortality despite his superhuman stature.

The relevance of Pedasos' mortality is made abundantly clear at lines XVI 466–471. While Patroclus is fighting in Achilles' stead and making use of his horses, Sarpedon throws a javelin at Patroclus:

Σαρπηδὼν δ' αὐτοῦ μὲν ἀπήμβροτε δουρὶ φαεινῷ
δεύτερον ὁρμηθείς, ὃ δὲ Πήδασον οὔτασεν ἵππον
ἔγχεϊ δεξιὸν ὦμον: ὃ δ' ἔβραχε θυμὸν ἀΐσθων,
κὰδ δ' ἔπεσ' ἐν κονίῃσι μακών, ἀπὸ δ' ἔπτατο θυμός.
δὲ διαστήτην, κρίκε δὲ ζυγόν, ἡνία δέ σφι
σύγχυτ', ἐπεὶ δὴ κεῖτο παρήορος ἐν κονίῃσι.

Sarpedon missed him with his shining spear as he rushed at him in turn, but he struck the horse Pedasos with his spear on the right shoulder, and the horse shrieked, gasping for life, and having bleated he fell down in the dust, and his spirit flew away. Then the other two sprang aside and the yoke creaked and the reins tangled, while the trace horse lay dead in the dust.

Iliad XVI 466–471

Pedasos' purpose, narratologically, is to die. Soon thereafter the immortal horses see Patroclus die as well, and as Zeus observes them shedding tears, he says:

ἃ δειλώ, τί σφῶϊ δόμεν Πηλῆϊ ἄνακτι
θνητῷ, ὑμεῖς δ' ἐστὸν ἀγήρω τ' ἀθανάτω τε;
ἦ ἵνα δυστήνοισι μετ' ἀνδράσιν ἄλγε' ἔχητον;

Oh wretched pair, why did we give you to lord Peleus, the mortal, you who are ageless and immortal? Was it so that you might have pains among miserable men?

Iliad XVII 443–445

These horses are also closely linked to Achilles' immortal mother, Thetis, because they were given to Peleus as a gift from the gods when Thetis was forced to marry him. The plight of these immortal horses next to a mortal companion and accompanied by mortal riders recalls the frequent lamentations of Thetis at having been forced to marry a mortal and to bear a mortal child whom she must see die. It is the plight of immortals who are close to morals. The unusual combination of mortal and immortal in Achilles' chariot team reflects the uneasy identity of Achilles himself, more than human but ultimately not fully divine. Pedasos' tragic demise foreshadows Achilles' own impending death as well as that of Patroclus, and we see that the *Iliad*'s tendency towards comparison of heroes and horses finds its most consistent expression in Achilles, the figure that is both most horse-like and most heroic.

Indic Horses and Indic Heroes

As we turn to Ṛgvedic evidence I should make clear that the genre of the Vedas is quite unlike that of the Greek epics. They are liturgical hymns without extended narrative and thus provide very different sorts of evidence, yet horses do feature prominently in them and their treatment is comparable. In the Vedas, for example, there is ample reference to horses' ability to share with humans the capacity for divinity. The Ṛgvedic corpus mentions no fewer than four immortal horses by name, Dadhikrā, Tarkṣya, Paidva, and Etaśa.[19] These, like the horses of Ares and the Dioskouroi, are all heavenly horses, but there is also a handful of Ṛgvedic hymns dedicated to horses that live among humans, namely the hymns to the sacrificial horse.

In approaching these hymns we should bear in mind how unusual they are, and the significance of that oddity. They occur in the Ṛgvedic corpus, which constitutes the earliest group of Vedic hymns. There are over a thousand of these hymns, and they almost exclusively praise divinities. The divine identity of the addressee is so expected that the addressee is referred to technically as the *devatā*, "divinity." The *devatā* of each hymn is specifically designated by commentators and constitutes one of the four categories by which Sanskrit commentaries consistently identify each hymn, others being the composer's name, the meter, and the hymn's ritual application. The *devatā* of these hymns is identified simply as *aśva*, "horse," according to this principle, which the commentator Sāyaṇācārya explains as follows: *aśvasya stūyamānatvādyā tenocyate sā devateti nyāyenāśvo devatā,* "because it is the horse who is being praised, the horse is the *devatā*, according to the principle that the *devatā* is that which is addressed by him [scil. the *ṛṣi*]."[20] His explication of this principle seems motivated by the oddity of a horse serving as the subject of a hymn, since this function is usually served by gods. In consideration of the fact that the corpus of

---

[19] MacDonnell 1898:148–149.
[20] Sāyaṇācārya, *ad Ṛgveda* I.162.

Ṛgvedic hymns does contain actual divine horses and that Ṛgvedic poetry and culture descend from an Indo-European tradition, in which horses may have been important religious symbols, it seems sensible to think that the capacity of the horse to function as the addressee of such a hymn in some way continues an Indo-European tradition of sacred and divine horses.

The content of *Ṛgveda* I.162 presents a tantalizing, if small, piece of evidence of this. The very first line of the hymn states: *vājíno devájātasya sápteḥ pravakṣyāmo vidáthe vīryáṇi;* "we proclaim in assembly the virtues of the prize-winning god-born horse."[21] Sāyaṇācārya does provide two synchronically feasible explanations for this: that horses were first born among the Gandharvas, a group of theriomorphic divine creatures, or that this has something to do with the first lines of the *Bṛhadāraṇyaka Upanishad*, which declare that the dawn of each day is the head of a horse and dusk its tail. Yet the fact that there were other examples of horses, or horse-like creatures, of supermortal status does not preclude the possibility that this, as well as other comparable phenomena, continues a pre-Indian tradition. Based on the presence of actual divine horses and the unusual role that horses can serve in Ṛgvedic hymns, it seems likely that the culture of the audience of the Ṛgvedic hymns accorded to horses an affinity to the immortal world that is more like that expected in humans than in other animals, much as the world of Homer does.

A further similarity of horses to heroes is also revealed by the very first word of the quoted passage, *vājin*, which is frequently used to describe horses in the *Ṛgveda*. I have translated the word as "prize-winning" to call to mind Homeric parallels, such as ἀθλοφόρος. The connotations of *vājin* presumably extend to horse racing, which can itself be a form of symbolic combat, but *vāja*, from which this adjective is derived, also indicates the loot taken from conquered enemies by a warrior. The Vedic hymn IV.38, to the immortal stallion Dadhikrā, directly compares him to a king, *nṛpatiḥ*, translated as "lord of men":

vājínam...dadhikrām...|
pruṣitápsum āśúṃ carkṛtyam aryó nṛpátiṃ ná śúram ||
yáṃ sīm ánu pravāteva drávantaṃ víśvaḥ pūrúr mádati hárṣamāṇaḥ |
...ghṛdhyantam medhayúṃ ná śúraṃ rathatúraṃ ||

prize-winning...Dadhikrā...dappled, swift, to be praised by the faithful man, like a lord of men himself, and valiant, at whom each man rejoices, glad at heart, while [Dadhikrā] runs as if down a precipice, striving, eager for the rewards of war, like a valiant charioteer.

Ṛgveda IV.38.2–4

---

[21] *Ṛgveda* I.162.1.

Kings in the context of the *Ṛgveda* are often praised as warriors, as they are in Homer, so *nṛpatiṃ*, the accusative form of *nṛpatiḥ*, here is a heroic epithet. This metaphor extends to describe Dadhikrā fighting in battle and snatching war spoils from enemies. Dadhikrā is propitiated in his capacity as hero, as, in fact, are the other divine horses, who are consistently described as invincible, vanquishers of chariots, etc. One of these immortal horses, Paidva, even takes the same epithet as Indra, *ahihan*, "dragon-slayer."[22] In the earliest literature of both Greece and India, then, horses and heroes are handled in notably similar ways and display a similar ontological positioning. In India too horses function as a reflection of the hero and are treated in ways that render them very much like heroes, while heroes are treated in ways that render them like horses. A fascinating manifestation of this overlap between horse and hero occurs in heroic names that involve horses.[23] While discussing these well-documented names, such as Vīśtāspa (Avestan "swift horse"), Puhvel argues convincingly that these names are not simply *bahuvrīhi* compounds that indicate possession, e.g. "he of whom there is a swift horse," but that they are meant to convey a sharing of quality between the horse and man. He says that "in onomastic usage the line gets blurred, even as 'Crazy Horse' hardly evokes the proud owner of a deranged equine."[24] The compounds indicate possession in a way that draws on the ability of one's horses to function as reflections of one's own identity with the result that the owner of swift horse possesses some of the qualities of a swift horse himself. Horse and hero, then, are equated on a poetic and onomastic level. If this tendency indeed reflects inherited PIE cultural practice, then the Greek poetic treatment of horse and hero may well be a more ancient and complex phenomenon than it first appears.

It could be argued, of course, that the evidence presented thus far does not preclude the possibility that these similarities simply reflect a coincidence of internal logic within these societies, i.e. heroes use horses in battle so the comparison of the two is simply natural and any overlap just the result of chance. Given the relationship between these cultures, in history and poetry, this would seem unlikely to me, but to bolster these conclusions one would want to see evidence of some kernel of this phenomenon in the parent culture as well. Since we have no literature from that culture, however, such evidence is inherently difficult to obtain, to say the least. In this particular instance, however, we may be in exceptionally good luck. This is so because of one particular element of IE religious practice that has to do with horses, to which I will now turn.

---

[22] *Ṛgveda* I.117.9, I.118.9.
[23] See the Introduction for a number of examples of this phenomenon, page 4.
[24] Puhvel 1987:269.

The Horse Sacrifice

The ritual wherein I seek corroboration of the antiquity of the phenomena discussed above is a horse sacrifice, a ritual that appears in multiple IE cultures with such similarity that it is regularly regarded as a reflection of religious practice in the parent culture. The issues surrounding this sacrifice are something of a *cause célèbre* among Indo-Europeanists, yet it may seem odd that it features in my own analysis of Homeric treatment of horses, because Greece is not, in fact, one of the places where this ritual was preserved.[25] I will argue, however, not that the ritual had direct influence on Greek poetic practice itself, but rather that the ritual sheds light on how the parent culture of Greece thought about horses and that features of this ideology regarding horses, if not its actual ritual practice, were inherited in Greece and affected Greek culture and poetry.

We must look then to the evidence for this kingly ritual, in which the space between equine and human identity became permeable, an appreciation of which has practical implications for our understanding of the unique treatment of heroes and horses in early Greek epic. The reconstruction of an actual religious ritual, however, is not as straightforward as the reconstruction of a word or phrase, and may not even be possible, because the evolution of a culture's religion does not progress by consistent or predictable tendencies. Therefore, although it is important here to review the evidence and even discuss at some length certain issues brought up in reconstruction, I will ultimately suggest that we should not try to reconstruct the ritual precisely, but instead examine what our evidence for it allows us to glimpse about the patterns of thought that shaped its formation generally. This, I think, will be more useful for the sort of analysis needed for the study of horses in Greek poetry and will help us avoid certain difficult pitfalls inherent to precise ritual reconstruction.

The most secure evidence for this sacrifice comes from ancient India and Ireland. Our evidence for a kingly horse sacrifice in India is extensive, comprising literary evidence as well as archaeological. The archaeological evidence includes an *aśvamedha* (horse-sacrifice) altar near Kalsi, inscriptions attesting performances of such sacrifices, [26] and even coinage.[27] Our literary evidence, however, provides the oldest and most thorough descriptions of the particulars of the ritual. There exist two Ṛgvedic hymns about the sacrifice, I.162 and I.163, and detailed information about the ritual procedure and associated mantras is also

---

[25] For early work see Dumont 1927; Koppers 1936; Negelein 1903. More recent bibliography will be cited throughout this section.

[26] Ramachandran 1951, 1952; Mirashi 1963:xx.

[27] Allan 1914:plate V.

provided by other texts, especially the *Śatapatha-brāhmaṇa*[28] and the *Śukla-yajur-veda*.[29] *Aśvamedhas* also occur in both the *Mahābhārata*, in book XIV, the *Aśvamedhikaparvan*, and in books I and VII of the *Rāmāyaṇa*. Puhvel provides a succinct summary of the ritual:

> The main ritual took three days. On the principal, second day of the sacrifice the king drove in a war chariot drawn by the stallion and three other horses. The victim was anointed by the king's three foremost wives, and its mane and tail were adorned with pearls....The stallion was smothered to death, whereupon the principal queen symbolically cohabited with it under covers, while the entourage engaged in obscene banter. Then followed the cutting up of the victim, disposal of the parts, further blood sacrifices, ablutions, and disbursement of priestly honoraria.[30]

The ritual could in fact be much more elaborate than this, and could involve as much as a full year of preparations, yet this summary will suffice for our current purposes.[31]

The Irish evidence comes from the twelfth-century Giraldus de Barri, known generally as Giraldus Cambrensis. He is the author of *Topographia Hibernica*. Although his depictions of the ancient Irish people are not at all flattering or unbiased, he describes a ritual in Kenelcunnil, in northern Ireland, that is similar enough to the *aśvamedha* that its basic veracity is usually accepted:

> Collecto in unum universo terrae illius populo, in medium producitur jumentum candidum. Ad quod sublimandus ille non in principem sed in beluam, non in regem sed exlegem, coram omnibus bestialiter accedens, non minus impudenter quam imprudenter se quoque bestiam profitetur. Et statim jumento interfecto, et frustatim in aqua decocto, in eadem aqua balneum ei paratur.

> When all of the people of that land had been gathered together, a white horse was led into the middle of them. He who is to be elevated not to a prince but a beast, not to a king but an exile, no less shamelessly than unwisely approaches that horse in the bestial fashion, in open sight of all, and professes himself to be a beast. The horse is then killed

---

[28] XIII.2.6.1–XIII.2.9.9; XIII.5.2.1–XIII.5.3.7.

[29] Vājasaneyi-saṃhitā XXIII. See also Śrauta-sūtra, Kātyayana-śrauta-sutra XX.5.1–XX.7.26.

[30] Puhvel 1987:271.

[31] A fuller description can be found in Fuchs 1996:17–28, and the authoritative and most exhausting account is Dumont 1927.

immediately and cooked in water, in which water a bath is prepared for the king.

O'Meara 1949:168

Regardless of any ethnic bias on the part of Giraldus, the details of this ritual seem too specific to be disregarded, and probably do reflect, at least in basic details, an actual ritual that is cognate with the *aśvamedha*.[32]

There is another, comparatively new piece of potential evidence that may strengthen this conclusion as well. In 1988, a large vase relief from İnandık was published by Özgüç.[33] The vase bears a series of friezes, and Watkins argues that these ought to be "read" from right to left and from bottom to top; this then would reveal a narrative of an elite man and woman led in a procession, at the end of which the couple are depicted as prepared to copulate *"in more ferarum."*[34] Unlike Özgüç, who thinks that the couple represents a god and goddess, Watkins argues that they are best understood as a king and queen and that this entire ritual may represent some remnant of a Hittite horse sacrifice that is cognate with the *aśvamedha*. If Watkins is correct, we have evidence here of a PIE ritual involving horse sacrifice and its association with kings in Ireland, India, and perhaps also in Anatolia. There is, thus, reason to surmise that this was an important rite in PIE culture.

While the details of the later rituals are not widely documented outside of India, there is enough information that some scholars have attempted to reconstruct at least the essential elements of the PIE rite.[35] It is, however, my opinion that such reconstructions are always in jeopardy of privileging one or another of the later traditions. Since the details of the Indian horse sacrifice are so much better documented than the others, one could easily be tempted to include elements of the Indian rite in the PIE reconstruction that are not justified by other sources. Some of the specially Indian procedures may indeed be genuine remnants of PIE ritual practice that have simply been lost elsewhere, but there is no way to know which these are, and thus these Indian practices cannot securely be assumed to have descended from PIE traditions. Additionally, actual ritual practice in the culture of the Proto-Indo-Europeans should not be expected to have been any more consistent than ritual practices in other

---

[32] Puhvel raises the possibility that a more accurate description of the ritual would have produced even more traces of PIE ancestry (1987:275). I will add that one key difference between the two rituals, the fact that one involves actual sexual contact and one does not, has been challenged by Jamison (1996:65), who argues that the Indian ritual did in fact contain sexual contact.

[33] Özgüç 1988.

[34] Watkins 1995:267.

[35] Dumézil 1954:73–91; Puhvel 1987:269–276; Doniger O'Flaherty 1980:149–212.

cultures, so as much room as is possible should be left in reconstructions for variations in ritual practice within PIE culture. Any such ritual is likely to have varied over time and even among different groups in the original community. Therefore, the safest methodology for hypothesizing about this particular ritual is to be minimalistic, using only the elements that are most secure and then to extrapolate from them a sense of the rationale of the sacrifice. This will undoubtedly give us an impression of the ritual that is unrealistically minimal, and we may suppose that in practice such sacrifices were much more elaborate than we can perceive. Yet it should provide us the surest details, which we will need in order to interpret early Greek poetic treatment of horses.

In such a minimalistic model many of the significant details of the later ritual will have to be omitted due to an inability to select between regional variants. Since my exclusion of some details is unusual I would like to explain the reasoning, before offering my conclusions. For instance, the Indian sacrifice involves the horse being killed by smothering before the copulation while the Irish tradition has it killed afterward in a manner that is unclear. Even more importantly, the Irish tradition has a king copulating with a horse, which should probably be assumed to be a mare, while the Indian tradition has a queen copulating with a stallion. It seems to me that the idiosyncrasies of these rituals are all so interrelated that it would be very difficult to select any particular facet of one ritual and project it all the way back to the parent culture. The method of execution in India, for example, is inextricably linked to the sequence of the ritual procedure there. It has occasionally been suggested that the explanation for this lies in the biology of asphyxia, in that death by asphyxiation gives rise to postmortem "tumescence," which may have been necessary for the ensuing procedures.[36] It seems better to assume that this method of killing is related to another notable distinction of the Indian procedure: the fact that the killing occurs before the ritual copulation. The fiction of living participation on the part of the horse is evident and, in fact, essential in all the ritual procedures. Throughout the entire drama of the *aśvamedha* ritual, the participants, who include at least three wives and several priests, pretend that the horse is alive. For example the queen utters once she has lain down with the dead horse, *ná mā nayati káścaná | sasastyaśvakáḥ*, "no one is leading me [euphemistically], the horsey is sleeping."[37] Furthermore there is no mantra associated with the killing of the horse, but this would, of course, have destroyed the fiction of the horse's life. Traditional methods of sacrifice would have precluded, or at least dramatically complicated, the maintenance of this fiction by leaving the body of the

---

[36] Puhvel 1987:272.
[37] Vājasaneyi-saṃhitā XXIII.18. My translation here is based on that of Jamison (1996:67).

animal visibly disfigured by the mortal wound. Thus the horse is presumably killed by smothering precisely because smothering leaves no marks. It is therefore necessary that the horse be killed before the sexual element of the ritual. If it were killed afterward, there would never be a need to pretend that the dead horse is alive, so no need for a method of execution that leaves no marks. This does not prove that the smothering could not have been part of the PIE ritual; it only requires that the smothering be tied to the ritual order: killing before sex.[38] To project the smothering onto the PIE ritual therefore requires that the ritual order be projected onto the PIE ritual as well. This is not, of course, impossible, but it is difficult to prove.[39] We cannot actually be sure then of how the horse was killed at all. My point is essentially that it is difficult to extricate this one or any one difference from a nexus of differences. If we attempt to create a terribly detailed reconstruction we are hard pressed not to retroject entire complexes of regional idiosyncrasies onto the parent culture.

We cannot be sure of the gender of the horse or even of the human participant. In our most useful bodies of comparanda, the Irish and the Indian, there is no agreement. The Hittite vase, if it does reflect a similar ritual, is of no help since both of these participants are human, perhaps playing the part of horses. In a lengthy treatment of the issue, Doniger O'Flaherty argues that the *aśvamedha* itself contains vestiges of a previous version of the ritual in which a man did indeed copulate with a mare. She points to a ready identification of the horse with the king, mediated by frequent solar symbolism which is pertinent to both figures, and focuses especially on the sexual abstinence, of both the king and the stallion, practiced during the preparation for the ceremony. [40] The stallion not only cannot have sex while the ritual is being prepared but, before his release for the year of wandering, is shown a pen of caged mares, whose sexually charged whinnying is a desirable omen. Doniger O'Flaherty sees in this caging and avoiding of female horses and women a symbolically manifested anxiety toward female sexual power. She sees these ancillary ritual elements as later, perhaps compensatory, additions to a ritual that had once had female sexuality

---

[38] If Doniger O'Flaherty should prove correct in her suggestion that the original sacrificial horse was a mare and that the killing of the horse before the ceremony is an Indian innovation to circumvent the difficulty, and danger, of compelling a stallion to mate with a human woman, then the smothering must be an attendant innovation. Doniger O'Flaherty 1980:149–212.

[39] Herodotus tells us at IV 71.4 of a Scythian practice in which a horse was sacrificed along with humans, one of which was a concubine who had been smothered. If this is true it is possible that this reflects a vestige of inherited IE sacrificial practice in which the smothering has been transferred from horse to human, but this is too speculative to include in my analysis above.

[40] The king is required to share a bed with his favorite wife but forbidden to have sex with her. This is presumably to be connected with the showing of the mares to the sacrificial stallion, who is also prevented from having sex for the entire year before the sacrifice.

as its principal feature. She argues that this may also explain the other principal difference between the two rituals, the fact that the horse is killed before the sexual act in the Indian version but after this act in the Irish. The switch from mare to stallion would make the horse the active, or penetrative, partner, and a live horse could not be counted on to perform this ritual function. The killing of the stallion and the subsequent fiction that the stallion is merely sleeping is a practical solution. Although this reasoning is tempting, I prefer to plot a more conservative course. I prefer to avoid most specific details entirely and to focus instead on the ritual logic of that sacrifice, the pattern of thought to which it testifies. In order to ensure the utmost stability of our analysis, I believe that no conclusion can safely be drawn as to the gender of the PIE horse without some agreement among our sources, and thus no safe conclusion can be drawn about either the ritual order of the death or the sex of the horse.

Despite these disagreements among the sources, however, some positive statements can be made about the PIE ritual. Our texts do agree that the king is understood to be a horse. In the Indian version, the horse and king are both meant to be sexually abstinent for a year, both being tempted by sex—the king by sleeping with his favorite wife and the stallion by being shown the penned-in mares. The sacrifice of the horse is also meant to renew the energy lost by the king. The horse also, of course, takes the place of the king in the sexual relationship with the queen. The Indian *aśvamedha* could have been performed for a variety of reasons, but in the *Rāmāyaṇa* it is performed because King Daśaratha cannot produce a child.[41] The queen's interaction with the horse allows the couple to have children. The horse is even called the *retodhā*, "semen-giver," and the command is given: *reto dadhātu*, "may it give the semen."[42] The horse stands in place of the king and by its death transfers to the king its power.

The Irish ceremony casts the king in a similar position. At first glance it seems odd that the king would declare himself to be a beast while having sex with a horse—and this is precisely the sort of thing that might not be trusted in Giraldus' account—yet it is what makes it most believable. For although the king is actually involved in this case and the animal is presumably a mare, the king's declaration that he himself is transformed into a horse is consistent with the *aśvamedha* in that the king is a horse in the logic of the sacrifice. Puhvel has even suggested that Giraldus may have mutilated a ritual declaration here that was similar to "I am stallion, you are mare," which may have cast this in the form

---

[41] The original purpose of the ritual is also a matter of inquiry. The fact that it helped to perpetuate a kingship seems secure, but whether its applications were more specific is not made clear from our sources. See Puhvel 1987:273–274.

[42] Vājasaneyi-saṃhitā XXIII.20.

of theriomorphic sacred marriage.[43] Whether or not this precise hypothesis is true, the Irish and Indian sources do agree in depicting the transformation of the king into a stallion and the queen into a mare. So long as this is secure, even if little else can be, substantial research can proceed.

The minimal, yet reliable deduction that we must work with, then, is that this evidence reflects a kingship ritual involving sex between a royal human and a horse, in which the king is identified with a stallion and the queen with a mare and in which the horse involved is killed at some point. The underlying ritual logic then is that of human/horse ontological overlap on a conceptual and ritualistic level.

There is one more piece of evidence for the Indian ritual which highlights the utility of relying only on the most minimalistic schematic regarding the actual ritual procedure. In addition to the archeological and literary evidence for the *aśvamedha*, there is also a non-Indian source. The eleventh-century Arab scholar Albêrûnî, who lived in India for much of his life, describes the ceremony as it apparently was practiced in his time. In his description there is no sex at all and the horse is a mare, yet the mare is still allowed to wander before the sacrifice just as the stallion was and, like the stallion, is followed by attendants. In this case, however, the attendants cry out as they follow her, "She is the king of the world. He who does not agree, let him come forward."[44] The ritual has probably been altered but could preserve some variant of the original that is simply undocumented otherwise. If the details of the ritual vary this much from the Vedic period to the eleventh century, then how much could they vary from the PIE to the Vedic? This example certainly demonstrates the need for caution in identifying the gender of the original victim, and the importance of prioritizing that which is secure, namely, a unique coincidence of human and equine identity in what is likely to have been a very culturally significant ritual.

Human Sacrifice and the Equus October

There is yet one more ritual that has often been suggested as a survival of the PIE horse sacrifice, that of the Roman Equus October. I have so far omitted it from this discussion because I do not think it is a direct descendant of that ritual, or least it cannot be confirmed as such. Yet it is worth discussing for two reasons. First, since other scholars have included it in their analysis, I ought to explain why I do not. Second, even though I think that it is impossible to prove a relationship to the ritual discussed above, it is nevertheless possible that

---

[43] Puhvel 1987:275.
[44] Trans. E.C. Sachau; Albêrûnî 2002:548.

practices concerning the Equus October still preserve evidence of early ideology regarding horses and humans that will be useful.

Our principal source is Festus, who says under his entry for "October Equus":[45]

> October equus appellatur, qui in campo Martio mense Octobri immolatur quotannis Marti, bigarum victricum dexterior. De cuius capite non levis contentio solebat esse inter Suburaneses et Sacravienses, ut hi in regiae pariete, illi ad turrim Mamiliam id figerent; eiusdemque coda tanta celeritate perfertur in regiam ut ex ea sanguis destillet in focum, participandae rei divinae gratia.

> The right-most horse of the winning chariot team is called the October horse and is killed each year in the field of Mars in the month of October. It is customary that no small fight occurs over its head between the Suburnians and Sacraviens; the former fight to hang the head on the wall of the regia, the latter on the Mamilian tower. The tail is carried to the Regia with such speed that its blood may drip into the hearth fire, for the sake of propitiating the goddess.

> Lindsay 1913:190

He also discusses it under his entry for *panibus*:

> Panibus redimibant caput equi immolati idibus Octobribus in campo Martio, quia id sacrificium fiebat ob frugum eventum; et equus potius quam bos immolabatur, quod hic bello, bos frugibus pariendus est aptus.

> They used to wreath the head of the sacrificed horse with loaves of bread on the Ides of October in the Campus Martius, because they made a sacrifice for the harvest of the crops. A horse was sacrificed instead of a bull because it [the horse] was better for war, the bull for the planting of crops.[46]

> Lindsay 1913:246

---

[45] For the full details of the argument for a cognate relationship, see Dumézil 1954:73–91.

[46] There is also a description from Polybius XII 4b: φησὶ τοὺς Ῥωμαίους ἔτι νῦν ὑπόμνημα ποιουμένους τῆς κατὰ τὸ Ἴλιον ἀπωλείας ἐν ἡμέρᾳ τινὶ κατακοντίζειν ἵππον πολεμιστὴν πρὸ τῆς πόλεως ἐν τῷ Κάμπῳ καλουμένῳ, διὰ τὸ τῆς Τροίας τὴν ἅλωσιν διὰ τὸν ἵππον γενέσθαι τὸν δούριον προσαγορευόμενον. "They say that the Romans even now commemorate the fall of Troy on a certain day by killing a war horse with a spear on the Campus because of the belief that the fall of Troy was brought about by a wooden horse."

Differences between this and the horse sacrifices discussed above are quite apparent. The ritual takes place annually while there is no evidence from the Indian or Irish versions that justifies understanding the PIE ritual as anything but a special occurrence rising out of particular circumstances. There is also no sex, which, it must be admitted, is a salient feature of the other rituals. There is also no real kingship involved. It seems then the Equus October is lacking in almost every requirement for inclusion in the group of IE horse sacrifices that descend from the PIE horse sacrifice. These differences have not, however, prevented scholars from seeing these rituals as related.

Most famously, Dumézil explained the majority of these differences as outgrowths of historical developments in Rome dealing with attitudes toward kingship.[47] As kingship disappeared from Roman society, the circumstances which had previously given rise to the PIE royal horse sacrifice could not occur. The ritual, he argues, may still have been preserved in an altered form due to its importance. This altered ritual could then have been made part of the regular Roman religious calendar and thus its performance assured. The fixing of the tail in the Regia, a site associated with Roman kingship from Numa onward, testifies, according to Dumézil, to the previously regal nature of the ceremony. He believed that the sexual nature of the ritual has been lost entirely, although Puhvel saw hints of it in the wish for fecundity indicated by the phrase *ob frugum eventum*.[48]

This is intriguing, and even tempting analysis, but it is not certain enough to warrant considering this ritual cognate with the *aśvamedha* and Irish rite at the moment. The substitution of the placement of a tail in the regia for sex with a king or queen is not convincing. It would be more convincing were the regia not the seat of Roman priestly authority. The fact that a ritual sacrifice has a connection to the home of the *pontifex maximus* is not odd enough to justify a special explanation. There is, then, neither sex nor a king, and, although there is a horse, there is no overlap of horse and human, which is the uniting theme of the Indian and Irish accounts.[49] Ultimately, the Equus October is not best understood as a descendant of the PIE horse sacrifice, at least not for our purposes.

---

[47] Dumézil 1954:73–91.

[48] Dumézil himself rejects this idea, arguing that this is an offering of thanks to Mars for defending the land and thereby allowing a successful harvest. The import of this phrase is entirely martial, he claims. Dumézil's vigorous critique is part and parcel of his broader critique of the possibility of an early "agrarian Mars," a version of the deity who wielded influence over agricultural affairs in addition to martial (1954:78 and 1966:221).

[49] A second Roman parallel to the *aśvamedha* has been suggested by Noonan (2006) in the form of the submersion of Mettius Curtius into the Lacus Curtius. Noonan argues that this submersion of the horse is related to the bathing of the horse prior to the Indian ritual. The bathing of the horse is indeed an important part of the Indian ritual and its procedure strictly prescribed, yet

Some utility may still be found in it, however, if we examine it for traces of inherited ideology concerning horses and sacrifice rather than for evidence relating to one horse sacrifice ritual in particular. For this I will point to an interesting and somewhat arcane feature of Indian sacrificial literature, the human sacrifice. The ritual is known as the *puruṣamedha* or *naramedha*, "human-sacrifice" and "man-sacrifice." It is unclear whether this ritual ever actually occurred or if it is a liturgical pretense, but its description in the *Śāṅkhāyana Srauta* presents a sacrificial practice that is modeled on the *aśvamedha*. Just like the horse, the human victim is allowed to wander for a year and is sacrificed along with a goat, and the chief wife of the king then engages in sexual contact with him.[50] Whether or not the ritual was actually performed, it seems to have been thought logical that horses and men would be sacrificed in the same very special way.[51]

This is potentially relevant in Rome and to the Equus October specifically only because, although there is no evidence of human sacrifice in Rome, there was a certain execution that was modeled on the Equus October. In 46 BC Julius Caesar, once a pontifex maximus, had mutineers decapitated in the Campus Martius and their heads hung up in the Regia, an odd procedure that is reminiscent of the sacrifice. Cassius Dio tells us that this was, in fact, done precisely in the manner of a sacrifice, and the Equus October seems to be the sacrifice that is implied:

ἄλλοι δὲ δύο ἄνδρες ἐν τρόπῳ τινὶ ἱερουργίας ἐσφάγησαν. καὶ τὸ μὲν αἴτιον οὐκ ἔχω εἰπεῖν (οὔτε γὰρ ἡ Σίβυλλα ἔχρησεν, οὔτ' ἄλλο τι τοιοῦτο λόγιον ἐγένετο), ἐν δ' οὖν τῷ Ἀρείῳ πεδίῳ πρός τε τῶν ποντιφίκων καὶ πρὸς τοῦ ἱερέως τοῦ Ἄρεως ἐτύθησαν, καὶ αἵ γε κεφαλαὶ αὐτῶν πρὸς τὸ βασίλειον ἀνετέθησαν.

The other two men were slaughtered in the manner of a sacrifice. I am not able to explain the reason for this, for the Sibyl did not order it nor was there any other such oracle. They were sacrificed in the Campus Martius by the pontifices and the priest of Ares [*flamen martialis*] and their heads were dedicated at the Regia.

Cassius Dio XLIII 24.4–5

---

without testimony in the Irish account, it cannot be taken for granted in the PIE ritual and therefore the possibility of a cognate in the Lacus Curtius incident, though tantalizing, must also, at least for the moment, be omitted from our analysis as it also does not involve sex, kingship, or hippomorphism.

50 For fuller description see Fuchs 1996:28.

51 See Puhvel 1978 on the hierarchy of sacrificial animals in the PIE world and the possible place of humans in it.

I do not claim that this reflects a shared methodology for human sacrifice in Rome and India at all, of course. I only point out that in each case, when a human sacrifice was imagined the logical ritual practice on which to model it was the sacrifice of a horse. The fact that horses occupied an ontological position that was closer to humans than other animals marked horse sacrifice as the most logical paradigm for human sacrifice. Even without direct relation then, the rituals may still testify to a similar ideological connection between horses and humans, an ideological connection that is a genuine inheritance, and that we have seen in our Greek poetic sources as well.

Again, it may be more useful to inspect ritual rationale than actual procedure, at least in this case and in this particular investigation. Such an approach allows us to look past the conflicting elements of our evidence. It allows us to observe a propensity toward a conceptual overlap of equine and human identity in the parent culture that was prominent in sacrifice.[52] We can see in the important kingly ritual, in fact, exactly the type of overlap of horse and hero in the parent culture that we needed to help us contextualize the overlap that we see in Greek poetic treatments of heroes and their horses, and that I have posited as a reflection of inherited ideology.

Horse Sacrifice in Greece

We should not conclude this discussion of horse sacrifice without addressing the realities of the practice in Greece. As in Rome, horse sacrifice was quite rare but did exist in ancient Greece, and appears in Greek literature as well as in the archaeological record. No Greek sacrifice resembles the IE kingly sacrifice, as argued above, but we do not need to restrict our discussion to confirmed ritual descendants.[53] For although there is no ritual in Greece of which I am aware that resembles the IE ritual, there are cultic and mythological vestiges of the nexus of hippomorphism, sex, and kingly power that reflect the ideology observed in the parent culture.

The fact that horse sacrifice is rare in Greece is not particularly surprising when one considers the fact that the eating of horse meat was taboo there,[54] and that sacrifices were in many ways religiously charged communal banquets.

---

[52] Gamkrelidze and Ivanov (1995) cite others rituals throughout the IE world that may testify this connection as well (402–403, 468, 469). They also discuss some Hittite law codes that treat humans and horses in similar ways (402, 464).

[53] It is tempting to assume from this fact that horse sacrifice was rare in the IE cultures in general, yet this would not be entirely true. The Persians may have sacrificed horses to the sun regularly, and horse sacrifices among the Germanic peoples do not seem to have been uncommon. For a list of other horse sacrifices in the IE world, see Dumont 1927:xv.

[54] Koppers 1936:292.

Thus, animals would not usually be sacrificed that would not then be eaten, a fact that shapes the Aeschylean description of the horror of human sacrifice in the case of the sacrifice of Iphigenia: θυσίαν ἑτέραν ἄνομόν τιν᾽, <u>ἄδαιτον</u>, "another sacrifice, unlawful, <u>not to be eaten.</u>"[55] This reluctance of Greeks to eat horsemeat, in apparent distinction from their PIE ancestors and Indian counterparts, even seems to have influenced the repartee between Hesiod and Homer in their legendary *Certamen*, in which Hesiod composes one line of verse and Homer has to compose the next. Hesiod composed lines for which it would be logically difficult to compose a companion line. In one instance, that difficulty seems to involve the taboo concerning the consumption of horse meat: Δεῖπνον ἔπειθ᾽ εἵλοντο βοῶν κρέα καὐχένας ἵππων, 107. This would lead the listener to expect the meat of the cows *and* the necks of the horses to be part of the meal. Finishing this line is a challenge because of the way that it plays on the cultural taboo of horse-eating. Homer, then, is quite deft to finish the couplet in a way that circumvents this problem with the line: ἔκλυον ἱδρώοντας, ἐπεὶ πολέμοιο κορέσθην, 108. This, then, renders the entire couplet as "they feasted on the meat of the cows and they loosed the sweating necks of the horses, since they had had their fill of war."[56]

Homer's need to alter the apparent semantic trajectory of the line grows partially out of the Greek disinclination to eat horse meat, but also coincides with a general unwillingness to sacrifice horses. It may, of course, seem odd that an animal that was once specially marked for important sacrifices becomes particularly unlikely as sacrificial victim. This need not be surprising, however, since it is possible that resistance to sacrificing a particular animal is paradoxically not unlike eagerness to sacrifice a particular animal. Each case reflects a designation of that animal as uniquely sacred. It is not hard to imagine the same reverence for an animal rendering it especially sacrificial in one time period and especially unfit for sacrifice in another. This very phenomenon is, in fact, evident in the transition from Vedic to post-Vedic attitudes toward the sacrifice of cows.

Horse sacrifice in Greece is not, however, completely unknown so much as uncommon.[57] There are, in fact, fascinating and potentially relevant references

---

[55] *Agamemnon* 151.

[56] The line is a clever manipulation of an Iliadic line, itself from a feast scene: οἱ δ᾽ ἵππους μὲν λῦσαν ὑπὸ ζυγοῦ ἱδρώοντας, "and they loosed from the yoke the sweating horses" (VIII 543).

[57] See Farnell 1977:4.13 and Kosmetatou 1993 concerning the evidence that we have for horse sacrifices from the Mycenaean period onward. It is sometimes said that Greeks made much less use of horses than their IE relatives because of the degree to which seafaring replaced agricultural production and land travel in Greece. This may also have influenced the relative paucity of horse-based religious symbolism. I would point out that the horse sacrifices that are documented in Greece occur most frequently in the central Peloponnese, where seafaring was less

to horse sacrifices being performed to Poseidon Hippios in commemoration of his coupling with Demeter in the form of a horse herself, which was discussed above. Recall that she, in her wandering in search of her daughter, was pursued by Poseidon and took on the form of a horse to escape him. He chased her, in the form of a horse himself, and eventually he had sex with her. Whether these sacrifices or the myths that surround them have any relationship to the *aśvamedha* is certainly not secure. The Indian and Irish comparanda provide the essential elements needed for identification in the ritual itself, while in this case these elements appear partly in the ritual itself and partly in its mythological etymology. That is to say that the sex and hippomorphism are not in the ritual but in the myth that *informs* the ritual. It is not impossible that the PIE horse sacrifice was itself linked to a mythological etymon which is uniquely preserved in the myth associated here; Doniger O'Flaherty has, in fact, argued for just such a possibility.[58] I will not claim that this mythology ought to be treated as the continuation of cognate tradition without hesitation (and it certainly should not be used to inform our reconstruction of the PIE ritual) but it does reflect an overlap in ideology, that of hippomorphic transformation and sex.

Additionally, there is a sacrifice of a horse mentioned by Pausanias that, although not much like the Indian or Irish accounts, does contain some important links to kingship and to the *Iliad*. He mentions the peculiar existence in Sparta of a grave marker for a horse which was sacrificed at the gathering of the kings of Greece to compete over Helen:

Ἵππου καλούμενον μνῆμά ἐστι. Τυνδάρεως γὰρ θύσας ἐνταῦθα ἵππον τοὺς Ἑλένης ἐξώρκου μνηστῆρας ἱστὰς ἐπὶ τοῦ ἵππου τῶν τομίων· ὁ δὲ ὅρκος ἦν Ἑλένῃ καὶ τῷ γῆμαι προκριθέντι Ἑλένην ἀμυνεῖν ἀδικουμένοις· ἐξορκώσας δὲ τὸν ἵππον κατώρυξεν ἐνταῦθα.

It is the so-called Grave of the Horse. For Tyndareus sacrificed a horse there and made the suitors of Helen swear an oath standing on the entrails of the horse. The oath was to protect from harm Helen and whoever was chosen to marry her. Having administered the oath he buried the horse there.

Pausanias III 20.9

important than in many other parts of Greece. The Spartans, who did perform horse sacrifices, specially worshiped the Dioskouroi, the divine horsemen, and worshiped Artemis with hippomorphic votive offerings. Festus himself cites, as a possible antecedent for the Equus October, the sacrifice of a horse by the Spartans offered to the winds at Taygetus.

[58] Doniger O'Flaherty 1980:149–152.

Although this bears no obvious relationship to the PIE ritual, there was perhaps in ancient Greece some connection between kingship and horse sacrifice. These were all kings who were gathered, and the man selected to marry Helen would become the king of Sparta.[59] Again, we see a continuity of ideology, preserved here in legend rather than in ritual.

Another Greek horse sacrifice must be mentioned due to its obvious prominence, even if it is difficult to interpret. The legendary Trojan Horse may be best understood as a horse sacrifice. The horse was offered by the Greeks to the Trojans and brought inside to be presented to the goddess at her sanctuary, as a sacrifice would have been. Burkert points out that the striking of the horse with a spear by Laocoön seems to reflect a sacrificial rite and even hints that this element may preserve, in altered form, an earlier, more explicitly sacrificial version of the story.[60] This idea seems to have been readily accepted in ancient Rome, since Festus says that the common belief at Rome was that the historic origin of the Equus October lay in the slaughter of a horse in retribution for the horse that brought about the fall of Troy, the mythical homeland of the Romans.[61] The sacrifice of the horse with a spear, like the one used by Laocoön, must have either developed from this belief, or at least given credence to it.

Finally, Odysseus, the devisor of the strategy, is himself sometimes said to have been transformed into a horse.

ὅτι τὸ μὲν τῶν φαλαγγίων καὶ ὄφεων γένος Τιτήνων ἐνέπουσιν ἀφ' αἵματος ἐζωγονῆσθαι, τὸν δὲ Πήγασον λαιμοτομηθείσης τῆς Γοργόνος ἀπὸ τῆς κεφαλῆς ἐκθορεῖν, καὶ οἱ μὲν Διομήδους ἑταῖροι εἰς θαλασσίους μετέβαλον ὄρνις, ὁ δὲ Ὀδυσσεὺς εἰς ἵππον, ἡ δὲ Ἑκάβη εἰς κύνα.

They say that the species of venous spiders and snakes were born alive from the blood of the Titans, and that Pegasos leaped forth from head of the Gorgon after her throat had been cut, and that the companions of Diomedes were changed into sea birds, Odysseus into a horse, and Hecabe into a dog.[62]

Sextus *Πρὸς Μαθηματικούς* I 264–265

---

[59] Pindar's fourth Olympian ode also contains a description of Zeus, the god of kings, that is noteworthy in this context: ἐπεί νιν αἰνέω, μάλα μὲν τροφαῖς ἑτοῖμον ἵππων, "Since I praise him, he who is very ready in the raising of horses" (14).

[60] *Aeneid* II 50–53; *Odyssey* viii 507; Burkert 1983:158–161.

[61] Polybius confirms that this was indeed a common Roman explanation for the origin of the Equus October ritual; See XII 4b.

[62] See also Sextus *Πρὸς Μαθηματικούς* 1.267, wherein appears the report that Odysseus died after being turned into a horse, ὅτι εἰς ἵππον μετέβαλε τὴν μορφήν.

Sextus mentions this story in the midst of a condemnation of what he saw as widespread scholarly reluctance to distinguish fact from fiction. Although Sextus mentions this story as if it was a normal topic of discussion among the educated, the obscurity of the other accounts among which it is mentioned may lead us to think otherwise. There are, however, other sources for this story. We find some corroborating data, for example, in Ptolemaios Chennos, who retells some useful pieces of information which, he claims, come from Herodotus:

Καὶ ὡς ἐν Τυρρηνίᾳ φασὶν εἶναι Ἀλὸς πύργον καλούμενον, ὀνομασθῆναι δὲ ἀπὸ Ἀλὸς Τυρρηνῆς φαρμακίδος, ἢ Κίρκης θεράπαινα γενομένη διέδρα τῆς δεσποίνης. Πρὸς ταύτην δέ φησι παραγενόμενον τὸν Ὀδυσσέα εἰς ἵππον μετέβαλε τοῖς φαρμάκοις καὶ ἔτρεφε παρ' ἑαυτῇ ἕως γηράσας ἐτελεύτησεν.

And in the Tyrrhenian land they say that there is a tower of the Sea and that its name comes from a Tyrrhenian poisoner, "Sea," who was a servant of Circe but who had left her mistress. He [Herodotus] says that when Odysseus came to her she turned him into a horse and looked after him until he died in old age.

Ptolemaios *apud* Photius *Bibliotheca* 150a16

Finally, we learn from Servius that Odysseus is said to have died when he, still in the form of a horse, was stabbed with a spear.

Necatur autem vel senectute, vel Telegoni filii manu aculeo marinae bel-vae extinctus. Dicitur enim, cum continuo fugeret, a Minerva in equum mutatus.

He was killed either by old age or by the spine of a marine creature at the hand of his son Telegonus. For he is said to have been turned into a horse by Minerva as soon as he fled.

Servius *auct. Aeneid* II 44

This particular source is especially tantalizing since the transformation is mentioned here as part of an essential, and fairly minimal, biography of the epic hero, as if this transformation was not terribly obscure to Servius. These scant bits of evidence, however, do not allow us to piece together a mythic narrative, nor even to be certain that they refer to the same story. They may, after all, simply refer to mythical variants linked through the common motif of Odysseus' equine transformation. Even without an overarching narrative, however, it is still evident that Odysseus was said to have been the subject of equine transformation and that, at least according to Servius, he was sometimes said to have been killed while in horse form, stabbed in a way not dissimilar to Laocoön's stabbing of the Trojan Horse.

In this last account, just as Burkert suggests, Odysseus seems to have been equated with the Trojan Horse itself, and the entire Trojan Horse episode seems to contain reflections of a horse sacrifice. I do not wish to suggest that this links the scene with the PIE ritual, of course, but it does suggest some history of horse sacrifice in the ancient Greek consciousness and, perhaps, the connection of horse sacrifices to transitions of power, an association that may have been inherent in the PIE ritual as well. It also bears further testimony to the existence of hippomorphism in Greek folklore. Other examples considered so far include the story of the hippomorphism of Demeter and Poseidon and an alternative genealogy of Achilles' immortal horses, who are said by Diodorus Siculus to be hippomorphized Titans.[63]

It seems then that Indian and Irish horse sacrifice rituals provide sufficient evidence for assuming that speakers of Proto-Indo-European performed a kingship ritual in which the human participant, or participants, was imagined as undergoing a hippomorphic change of some sort. Our Greek evidence, additionally, provides evidence that a mythology of the hippomorphizing of humans and the connection of horses to kingship were still active in ancient Greek culture as well.[64] It may therefore be inferred that the existence of these concepts in the PIE tradition had some influence on depictions of Greek heroes, who were of course warrior-kings, compared to and ontologically linked to horses, themselves ontologically similar to humans, especially heroic humans.

Finally, as discussed above about India and potentially Rome, the depiction of human sacrifice in Greece can provide useful evidence to confirm this continuity of ideology. Our Greek evidence does not provide an obvious cognate with the Indian ritual but, again, presents a few important pieces of evidence.[65] The seventh-century burial at Lefkandi, for example, is often seen to document a human sacrifice, a *satī*, that may have accompanied the sacrifice of horses.[66] Greek literature provides evidence as well, in at least two prominent forms.

---

[63] See page 43, note 18.

[64] The association between horses and kingship must have also been influenced by the expense required to maintain horses and the useful role of horses in displaying one's wealth; cf. Griffith 2006. It is the son's love for horses in Aristophanes' *Clouds* that serves as touchstone for the economic and class anxiety of the work. In both Athens and Rome classes of rich men were designated as horsemen, the Hippeis and the Equites. The economic and social signification of horses is also documented by the use of equestrian statues for self-representation and aggrandizement among the wealthy.

[65] For a full treatment of human sacrifice in Greece see Hughes 1991.

[66] Hughes 1991:46–47.

The first comes in Achilles' sacrifice of twelve Trojan youths at the funeral of Patroclus, at which the youths are hurled into the fire. This sacrifice is particularly interesting because it is accompanied by the slaughter of πίσυρας ἵππους ἐριαύχενας, "four strong-necked horses."[67] Other animals were sacrificed as well, but it is the horses and the men to whom Achilles draws attention as he tells the other Greeks to remove the bones of Patroclus from the pyre. He says that Patroclus' bones will be easy to distinguish because they are apart from the rest, which are ἐπιμὶξ ἵπποι τε καὶ ἄνδρες, "the horse and the men mixed together."[68] Additionally, the dressing of the victims for the sacrifice is explicitly mentioned for the other animals, yet the horses and men are simply "thrown" on the pyre.[69] It is not impossible that the slaughter of the men and horses should be understood as having occurred before they are thrown on the fire, but it does seem as if they were thrown on alive. If this is true, the horses and men are treated in a uniquely similar way and truly marked out from the other victims.

It can be argued that this constitutes an actual sacrifice to the dead Patroclus, or that it simply results from an overflow of Achilles' fury, but in either case it is contextualized by Achilles' desecration of the corpse of Hector as part of a general pattern of grief-induced sacrilege. Although horses were, on occasion, sacrificed in some parts of ancient Greece, they were not a regular sacrificial animal, and in the context of the *Iliad* it seems that the slaughter of the horses somehow parallels that of the youths and that both reflect the quality of Achilles' transgressive behavior. The sacrifice of humans is again modeled on the sacrifice of horses.[70]

Both in the actual liturgy of the *puruṣamedha* and in several other notable sacrifices in the PIE world there is a tendency to compare humans to horses. I believe that this preserves an inherited tendency toward the hippomorphizing of humans and anthropomorphizing of horses that is linked to a conceptual overlap of the species that is traceable to prehistoric times and the common culture of the Indo-European peoples. To return to the epic heroes, then, the similarity between horses and heroes reflected in both our Greek and our Vedic Sanskrit sources is not a fully isolated phenomenon, but one special realization of a broader tendency, one that is evident not only in our literary sources but in sacrificial practices continuous from distant antiquity.

---

[67] *Iliad* XXIII 171.
[68] *Iliad* XXIII 242.
[69] *Iliad* XXIII 161–178.
[70] Burkert (1983:159) suggests that the killing of Odysseus casts him as the sacrificed Trojan Horse and links the barb with which he was killed with the spear used by Laocoön to pierce the wooden horse. If this analysis is correct then this episode also reflects the pattern outlined above.

The Horse Sacrifice and the Life of Pelopidas

The horse sacrifice described in Plutarch's *Life of Pelopidas* may bear special testimony to the ideological nexus described above. Since the passage has never, to my knowledge, been analyzed in the light of IE horse sacrifices, I think that it is worthwhile to attempt to examine it through the information presented above. The Greek legends of the Leuktridai and of the sacrifice offered to them on the eve of the Theban battle against the Spartans in 371 BCE contain descriptions of a horse sacrifice that is very infrequently discussed in scholarly studies but incredibly interesting in light of the PIE horse sacrifice and the symbolic logic between humans and horses to which it testifies. It does not, I think, constitute a direct Greek descendant of the famous PIE ritual, but it does reflect categories of ideological inheritance outlined above.

Elements of the story are scattered across numerous sources, and few of these agree in exact detail, but a composite of the texts presents enough common features to allow construction of a basic narrative.[71] Sisters known as the Leuktridai lived somewhere near the Leuktrian plain.[72] These girls are usually two in number, and their names, when given, are Molpia and Hippo, Melitia and Hippo, or Thano and Euxippe. Despite some disagreement, one of their names is consistently hippologicial (Hippo and Euxippe).[73] These women were raped by Spartan men and subsequently died by their own hands, according to most accounts.[74] The site of their death was then prophesied to be the future setting of a Spartan military defeat. This eventually came to pass in 371, when the Spartans faced the Thebans.[75]

Pausanias and Plutarch both relate that on the eve of that battle a sacrifice was performed in honor of the girls. Pausanias offers no details about the nature of the sacrifice, but Plutarch says in two passages that it was a horse sacrifice

---

[71] For a full review of potential sources see Schachter 1981:2.122. The principal ancient sources are Ailianos fr. 77; Diodorus Siculus XV 54.2–3; Pausanias IX 13.5–6, 14.3; Plutarch *Life of Pelopidas* 20–22, *Amatoriae Narrationes* 773B–774D, *De Herodoti Malignitate* 856F; Xenophon *Hellenika* VI 4.7.

[72] The origin of this name is itself disputed by our sources: they are sometimes said to be the descendants of a man named Leuktros, but otherwise they are the daughters of Skedasos, in which case their name must derive from their place of origin. Pausanias claims that they are the daughters of Skedasos. Both Plutarch's *Life of Pelopidas* and the *Amatoriae Narrationes* call them the daughters of Skedasos, while *De Herodoti Malignitate* calls them the daughters of Leuktros. Diodorus says that they were the daughters of both men.

[73] It is difficult to observe the name Leuktridai and the girls' equine names and not think of the λεύκιπποι, or bright horses, the sons of Zeus who are generally thought to be the Greek manifestation of the IE divine horsemen. It seems safest to me, however, to treat this as coincidence.

[74] In the *Amatoriae Narrationes* they are murdered by the Spartans. Their father is often said to have taken his own life as well.

[75] See Fontenrose on the relevant Delphic prophesies, 146–148.

and that it was requested by an image of the girls' father that appeared to the Theban general in a dream. In the *Amatoriae Narrationes* (774D), Plutarch says that it was a white horse. He does not specify the age or gender of the horse but simply calls it a ἵππος, which may refer to either a mare or stallion. The *Life of Pelopidas* is much more detailed and differs markedly in the color of the horse:[76]

Ὁ δὲ Πελοπίδας ἐν τῷ στρατοπέδῳ κατακοιμηθεὶς ἔδοξε τάς τε παῖδας ὁρᾶν περὶ τὰ μνήματα θρηνούσας καὶ καταρωμένας τοῖς Σπαρτιάταις, τόν τε Σκέδασον κελεύοντα ταῖς κόραις σφαγιάσαι παρθένον ξανθήν, εἰ βούλοιτο τῶν πολεμίων ἐπικρατῆσαι....πῶλος ἐξ ἀγέλης ἀποφυγοῦσα καὶ φερομένη διὰ τῶν ὅπλων, ὡς ἦν θέουσα κατ' αὐτοὺς ἐκείνους, ἐπέστη· καὶ τοῖς μὲν ἄλλοις θέαν παρεῖχεν ἥ τε χρόα στίλβουσα τῆς χαίτης πυρσότατον, ἥ τε γαυρότης καὶ τὸ σοβαρὸν καὶ τεθαρρηκὸς τῆς φωνῆς· Θεόκριτος δ' ὁ μάντις συμφρονήσας ἀνεβόησε πρὸς τὸν Πελοπίδαν· ἥκει σοι τὸ ἱερεῖον ὦ δαιμόνιε, καὶ παρθένον ἄλλην μὴ περιμένωμεν, ἀλλὰ χρῶ δεξάμενος ἣν ὁ θεὸς δίδωσιν.

When Pelopidas lay down to sleep in the camp he seemed to behold these girls weeping over their tombs and cursing the Spartans. He also saw Skedasos [their father] commanding him to sacrifice to the girls a red-haired maiden, if he desired victory over his enemies....A filly broke away from a herd of horses and ran through the camp, and when it had run right up to them, it stood still. While the rest of the men were admiring the shining fiery color of her mane, and her exultant nature, as well as the vehemence and boldness of her voice, Theokritos, the seer, reflected and cried out to Pelopidas, "Your sacrifice has come, sir. Let us not wait for another maiden, but accept and use the one that the god offers."

Plutarch's Life of Pelopidas 21–22

The sacrifice was then made and the Thebans went on to victory.

The relevance of the discussion to this particular scene is presumably clear. The horse here is not just sacrificed instead of a girl but as a girl. The seer makes this explicit, and the horse and girl are the same gender, both young (it is a πῶλος), and they both have the same color hair (παρθένον ξανθήν; χρόα

---

[76] More detail may be given in this account in order to contrast the character of Pelopidas with that of Agesilaus, who had a similar vision and with whose biography Plutarch's depiction of Pelopidas is paired. For commentary on this scene vis-à-vis Plutarch's generally see Georgiadou 1997:161–172 and Westlake 1939:13.

στίλβουσα τῆς χαίτης πυρσότατον).[77] The horse is sacrificed for girls who themselves have an equine element in their identity, at least onomastically, and the horse is offered as a substitute for a human girl whose identity it reflects. What we are seeing here is, in fact, sacrificial hippomorphism like that expressed in the Irish ritual, pervasive in the *aśvamedha*, and structural in the *puruṣamedha*. Even if this is not a real ritual it participates in the same logic that shaped the ancestral ritual. It is the same symbolic logic present in Achilles' killing of twelve young Trojan warriors and twelve horses in *Iliad* book XXIII. This sacrifice does not deal with kingship, but it does deal with political power and patriarchal authority, as the *aśvamedha* does. There is no equine sex, but there is sexualization of different sorts, both in the initial rape and perhaps in the character of the girl and horse, or girl/horse, whose youth, gender, and general visual allure are erotically colored. Although this is clearly not a literal ritual continuation of the PIE horse sacrifice itself, it reflects the same ideological nexus that informed that ritual.

Early in this chapter I attempted to highlight a species boundary that is implicit in early Greek poetry, one that separates humans and horses from other animals. The existence of this boundary has widespread ramifications in Greek literature and informs human and equine poetic comparisons as well as mythical examples of hippomorphism. The fact that many of these phenomena are reflected in the related poetry and culture of India, as well as in other IE cultures, led me to propose that these are not purely Greek developments but instead local outgrowths of an ancient cultural ideology, inherited in Greece and common to other IE cultures. As proof of this I pointed to evidence concerning horse sacrifices in Greece and elsewhere. For in these rituals we find evidence of this phenomenon and proof that it appeared not just in daughter cultures but in the parent culture as well. Not only do we have evidence that an ontological overlap of horse and human was central to the kingly horse sacrifice, but even our human sacrifice texts seem to imagine human sacrifice as modeled on horse sacrifice specifically, in Greece as well as in related cultures. We have good reason to believe, then, that Greek mythic and poetic treatment of horses and humans developed out of inherited cultural tendencies.

---

[77] It will be shown in Chapter 3 that hair is a very common focus in comparisons of human and equine form, especially in the case of eroticized comparisons.

3

Lyric Horses

I believe that it is clear that the PIE horse sacrifice ritual and the depiction of the hero in Greek epic reveal an inherited Indo-European tendency toward the hippomorphizing of humans and the anthropomorphizing of horses which continued to exert influence into the Greek Archaic period. The examples of this phenomenon that have been considered so far have focused generally, although not exclusively, on the similarities that are to be found between horses and epic heroes. Yet this tendency, epitomized in the PIE kingly horse sacrifice ritual, exerted influence on the poetic landscape beyond the epic battlefield. This is clear from the fact that hippomorphic depictions of humans are especially common in Greek lyric. These depictions, however, are often of a very different tenor from those of epic and point up a different set of similarities in the ancient Greek conceptions of horses and humans. The points of coincidence in lyric depictions of horses and humans are largely erotic and present the beauty of horses as uniquely analogous to the beauty of humans, and also draw heavily from the symbology of sexual dominance inherent in horse-riding. These comparisons are especially important counterpoints to the description of horses examined in Chapter 2 because they often deal with women. As in the case of the heroic depictions of horses discussed in the previous chapter, aspects of these erotic depictions may have some precedent in the PIE horse sacrifice, in which the ability of the horse to stand as sexual substitute for a human is an essential component.

By looking at the ways in which horses function in depictions of human sexuality, both male and female, I hope to situate the previous discussion of horses and heroes within a broader understanding of the poetic role that horses played in ancient Greece and also to draw out a fuller range of the hippomorphizing IE tendency, of which that involving heroes is just one facet. Many of the sources to be considered here are quite famous, and their imagery is well studied.[1] Yet I hope that after a review of these sources I will be able to present new angles from which to view them and new contexts in which to understand them. This sexualizing element of the treatment of horses in early Greek poetic art will, in fact, ultimately be shown to play a significant role in the development and deployment of early Greek metapoetry, namely in the image of the charioteer, a subject which will both conclude this chapter and form the backdrop for the next.

Women and Horses

Equine metaphors and hippomorphic depictions of humans are especially common in Greek lyric, indicative not only of martial excellence but also of erotic impulse. Since the erotic object of Greek lyric can be a male human just as easily as it can be a female, it is only logical that hippological depictions of human sexuality would have both male and female subjects. As mentioned in the last chapter, the PIE horse sacrifice comprises our best evidence for hippomorphism in the parent culture and none of our evidence regarding that sacrifice suggests any reason to expect that the phenomenon was restricted to men. Although the slippage of identity between horse and king seems to have been the most important aspect of the ritual, there was a concomitant transformation of mare and queen. The ritual logic was seen to rest upon a general ontological similarity and even overlap of humans and horses generally, so it is not surprising that the Greek daughter culture displays vestiges of that phenomenon in its depiction of women and men. Yet the conventions of ancient Greek sexuality do not yield an identical treatment of male and female sexual objectification, and male and female hippomorphically eroticized subjects are accordingly treated somewhat differently. I will first highlight some examples dealing with female subjects, and then move to examples involving males.

The most extensive example of hippomorphic erotic imagery in Greek literature is probably Alcman's *Partheneion*, which represents the most prolonged demonstration of this phenomenon in Greek lyric. This lyric is particularly interesting from the point of view of horses and gender because it is not only about women, but was also performed by women. It appears, in fact, to have been written for performance by a chorus of Spartan girls engaged in a choral

---

[1] An excellent analysis of the erotic associations of horses has been produced by Griffith (2006); for an extensive treatment of these themes from a non-IE perspective see esp. part II. In part because the erotic associations of horses in Greek poetry have been detailed elsewhere, my own documentation of the phenomenon will not be exhaustive. I will instead analyze prominent passages that are at once reflective of broad phenomena and most relevant to the comparative arguments advanced throughout this work.

competition. Although the lyric begins with the narration of local Spartan mythology, the ensuing dialogue is largely self-reflective, calling explicit attention to the qualities of the song and its performers, and contrasting those with the qualities of the opposing choruses.[2] The tone of these self-reflective moments is repeatedly erotic, and is probably also homoerotic, something not often attested between women in our ancient sources.[3] It is not perhaps surprising that the beauty of the girls in the competition is a frequent subject of the hymn, since Greek society would readily have allowed that the beauty of the performer justifiably influences the effectiveness of the performance, but it may be surprising that the beauty of the girls is repeatedly phrased in hippological terms:

Δοκεῖ γὰρ ἤμεν αὔτα
ἐκπρεπὴς τὼς ὥπερ αἴτις
ἐν βοτοῖς στάσειεν ἵππον
παγὸν ἀεθλοφόρον καναχάποδα[4]
τῶν ὑποπετριδίων ὀνείρων.

That one seems to stand out as when someone sets among the grazing beasts a strong, victorious, loud-footed horse, from one of the dreams under a rock.

Alcman *Partheneion* 45–49

As Campbell points out, this is strongly reminiscent of Homeric dactylic hexameter, although not dactylic itself, and recalls the Homeric phrase ἵππους / πηγοὺς ἀθλοφόρους; "strong prize-winning horses," *Iliad* IX 123–124.[5]

The competitive nature of the choral performance alone may seem enough to explain a hippological Homer reference, since the horses of the *Iliad* are readily indicative of combat, of which even nonviolent competition may be

---

[2] This is the most common understanding of the circumstances of the performance, but there are others. Several possibilities are discussed by Page (1951:52–57). Robbins (1994) has argued that there is, in fact, no other chorus and that the competitive imagery here only works to oppose the leaders of this one chorus to each other as well as to differentiate them from the girls whom they are leading.

[3] See Brooten 1996; Dover 1977:171–184.

[4] It should be noted that the epithet καναχάποδα, although not attested in the *Iliad*, is of some Homeric precedent in that it appears, in Ionic form, καναχήποδα, in the *Certamen*, 100. This resembles the phonetically related Homeric horse formulas discussed in Chapter 1. Although beyond the scope of that study, it is possible that the phenomenon studied there has reach beyond Homer and influenced non-Homeric equine poetic vocabulary.

[5] Campbell 1967:203.

seen as a form. Yet soon after this line, the other of the chorus leaders is also compared to a horse:

ἦ οὐχ ὁρῆς; ὁ μὲν κέλης
Ἐνητικός· ἁ δὲ χαίτα
τᾶς ἐμᾶς ἀνεψιᾶς
Ἁγησιχόρας ἐπανθεῖ
χρυσὸς [ὡ]ς ἀκήρατος·

Don't you see? The courser is Venetic, but my cousin Hagesichora's hair blooms like unmixed gold.[6]

Alcman *Partheneion* 50-54

This comparison is, I believe, without Homeric precedent. The competitive import of the courser is still felt, of course, but the introductory "ἦ οὐχ ὁρῆς;" hints that the visual beauty of the horse is relevant in much the same way as its speed and that both qualities are meant to reflect the competitive preeminence of the chorus leader. This is followed by a similar comparison that makes the importance of the performers' beauty explicit:

ἁ δὲ δευτέρα πεδ' Ἀγιδὼ τὸ ϝεῖδος
ἵππος Ἰβηνῶι Κολαξαῖος δραμήται·

The second horse after Agido in beauty will run [like] a Kolaxian after an Ibenian.

Alcman *Partheneion* 58-59

Although the metaphor here is clearly of a horse race and the competition among the girls is likened to that between competing horses, the beauty of the girls is the central point and the inferiority of this girl's beauty to Agido's seems to imply that she is inferior as chorus leader. The girls' capacity as choral performers is at least partially dependent on their sexual attractiveness, and horses are apparently fitting representatives of beauty that functions as an element of their competitive excellence.

The erotic connotations of horses may help to explain a certain point of interpretive controversy regarding the phrase ὑποπετριδίων ὀνείρων (49). I have translated this as "from one of the dreams under a rock," just as the text reads, but this understanding of the text is not universally shared. It is common

---

[6] It should be noted that the word χαίτα can refer both to human hair and to equine hair. This word is a prominent feature of human/horse comparisons and will be discussed shortly. For the fame of the Venetic horses in the ancient classical world, see Beaumont 1936.

to read ὑποπετριδίων as if it were ὑποπτεριδίων and thus the phrase would be understood to mean "from one of those winged dreams." Page, for example, translates the passage this way, but he does not alter the text, and cites the authority of the *Etymologicum Magnum*.[7] Page and the compiler of the lexicon presumably both prefer this interpretation for the same reason: ὑποπετριδίων ὀνείρων does not make clear sense. ὑποπτεριδίων ὀνείρων could be less problematic because dreams are occasionally described as having wings.[8] This conclusion requires, however, that one accept that an unexpected metathesis of the consonantal tau sound and the vocalic sound of the epsilon has occurred in this word in the Spartan dialect. Even if this phonetic development is acceptable, it is still not clear what these winged dreams have to do with horses. The reading "from one of those winged dreams" does not actually make significantly better sense than the obvious reading and is also linguistically problematic. Nagy, however, suggests a way of avoiding these pitfalls by demonstrating that the obvious reading may, in fact, have made perfect sense, by citing scholia that attest to a myth of Poseidon fathering the first horse through a nocturnal emission that occurred while he was sleeping under a rock. His emission then became the first horse:[9]

ἐπί τινος πέτρας κοιμηθεὶς ἀπεσπερμάτισε, καὶ τὸν
θορὸν δεξαμένη ἡ γῆ ἀνέδωκεν ἵππον πρῶτον[10]

Having fallen asleep on a rock, he ejaculated, and the earth, having received the semen, produced the first horse.

Scholia to Pindar *Pythian* IV 246

Thus, there is mythological precedent for translating the phrase as it appears. Furthermore this clearly reveals an association between horses and sexuality which would make very good sense in this lyric. If this reading is correct, it makes this association an explicit part of the symbology of the lyric. The inherent association of horses with sexuality is an important motivating force in the hippological comparisons used throughout this lyric.

It should be made clear that there is a general equine theme to the *Partheneion*. The lyric seems to have been written for a competition at the temple of Artemis Ortheia,[11] who was propitiated with hippomorphic votive

---

[7] Page 1951:87; *Etymologicum Magnum* 783.21.
[8] Page 1951:87.
[9] Although this story seems odd, it is not without parallel. Cf. the birth of Erechtheus from Hephaistos, Apollodorus *Library* III 14.6; Pausanias I 2.6.
[10] For further discussion of this and similar evidence, see Nagy 1990a:224–234; esp. 232.
[11] Dawkins 1926.

offerings.[12] Additionally, the lyric begins with a description of the myth of the descendants of Hippocoön, who were slain by the Dioskouroi. Hippocoön is not himself particularly associated with horses, at least not in a way that our limited sources for Spartan mythology allow us to know, but his very name is suggestive of equine associations. The Dioskouroi are consistently depicted as horsemen and associated closely with horsemanship. They are, in fact, often identified with the Indian *Aśvins*, or horsemen, and the IE Divine Twins.[13] We know virtually no details of the battle between the Dioskouroi and the Hippocoöntidae, but it seems that it pitted one group of horse-heroes against another. There is a hippological symbolic network here that extends beyond the choruses, and much of the hymn is concerned with horses in some way. The Spartans were renowned for their hippomania and especially noteworthy for the training of girls in horse-riding.[14] The erotic equine imagery coincides with the song's pervasive equine theme, but it is not born from the theme, as further examples will demonstrate. The song instead exploits a connection between horses and sexual attractiveness that was broadly culturally resonant.

Such hippomorphic depictions of attractive girls are not confined to Sparta, although the horse-raising culture of Sparta makes their use especially sensible there. Similar poetic tropes are recognizable elsewhere, as in a famous poem by Anacreon:

πῶλε Θρηικίη, τί δή μεν λοξὸν ὄμμασι βλέπουσα
νηλέως φεύγεις, δοκεῖς δέ μ’ οὐδὲν εἰδέναι σοφόν;
ἴσθι τοι, καλῶς μὲν ἄν τοι τὸν χαλινὸν ἐμβάλοιμι,
ἡνίας δ’ ἔχων στρέφοιμί σ’ ἀμφὶ τέρματα δρόμου·
νῦν δὲ λειμῶνάς τε βόσκεαι κοῦφά τε σκιρτῶσα παίζεις,
δεξιὸν γὰρ ἱπποπείρην οὐκ ἔχεις ἐπεμβάτην.[15]

Thracian filly, why do you look at me askance and run away pitilessly? Do I seem a fool to you? Well know this, I would skillfully throw the bridle on you and grabbing your reins turn you around the racetrack. Now you graze in the meadows and nimbly skip around in your play, for you do not yet have a skillful rider.

Anacreon 417

Clearly there is much more at work here than simply comparing the girl to a horse because of their shared beauty. The metaphor of the man's role in courtship as

---

[12] Dawkins 1926:146.
[13] For an extensive treatment of this and its ramifications in Greece see Frame 2009.
[14] Pomeroy 1975:19–24.
[15] Recall the sexual double entendre of the verb ἐπιβαίνω discussed in Chapter 1, page 18.

horse tamer is the dominant idea, yet this depends on, and in turn reinforces, the association between horses and sexuality and is surely also reliant on the beauty of young horses as emblematic of the beauty of young girls. In fact, the power dynamic assumed in ancient Greek erotic relationships is presumably an important part of the logic of the erotic hippomorphic comparisons. A significant part of taming a horse was and is "breaking" it for riding, and the metaphor of riding as sexual intercourse was common in Greek antiquity as it is contemporary culture.[16] The fact that a young horse required breaking is not an alternative explanation for the hippomorphic depictions of young girls but a complementary one. The breaking of the horse and the nature of its relationship to men cooperate in the phenomenon of hippomorphic imagery.

The first word of this lyric, πῶλος, is particularly interesting here in light of the discussion of Hades' epithet κλυτόπωλος in Chapter 1, and a potential allusion here to the *Homeric Hymn to Demeter*.[17] Anacreon's depiction of a young girl playing in a meadow, careless of the attention or sexual plan of her male viewer, calls to mind the Homeric image of Persephone picking flowers just before her abduction in the hymn:

παίζουσαν κούρῃσι σὺν Ὠκεανοῦ βαθυκόλποις,
ἄνθεά τ' αἰνυμένην ῥόδα καὶ κρόκον ἠδ' ἴα καλὰ
λειμῶν' ἂμ μαλακὸν

[He seized her] playing with the deep-bosomed daughters of Oceanus, and plucking flowers through the tender meadow, the rose, and the crocus and the lovely violets.

Homeric Hymn to Demeter 5–7

Anacreon describes the Thracian girl very similarly in line 5: νῦν δὲ λειμῶνάς τε βόσκεαι κοῦφά τε σκιρτῶσα παίζεις, "Now you graze in the meadows and nimbly skip around in your play."

As Anacreon relies here on the depiction of Persephone's abduction by Hades for the setting of this song it is remarkable that the girl is called a πῶλος, the very word at the core of the Homeric epithet κλυτόπωλος that proved confusing to scholars ancient and modern.[18] The immediate point of the image of the πῶλος here is, of course, to deploy the metaphor of horse-taming as a power-laden sexual act. Xenophon, in fact, tells us that the verb used in

---

[16] See Griffith 2006:324–325; Aristophanes *Lysistrata* 60.

[17] Cf. *Homeric Hymn to Demeter* 18.

[18] It is not strictly necessary that this be an actual allusion to the *Homeric Hymn to Demeter*, but could draw on poetic type-scenes dealing with sexual abduction generally. The fact that this scene recalled the abduction of Persephone is likely in either case.

describing the breaking of a horse is πωλυέειν and the man who breaks the horse is the πωλοδάμνης.[19] In the allusive context of Anacreon's lyric, however, it is hard not to think that πῶλος means something more.

I suggest that there is a sort of poetic humor at work here, based on a tradition of which we are unaware, in which this foal-breaking metaphor meets the intransparency of the epithet κλυτόπωλος and yields a solution that makes Persephone herself the πῶλος of the epithet. Persephone is, of course, the eternal bride, the ever-youthful κόρη, so she would be a perfectly logical subject of this equine metaphor. If this is true it would not be hard to see here a clever reinterpretation of κλυτόπωλος. As discussed earlier, Hades is not famous for his horses generally, and when his horses are described they are ἵπποι rather than πῶλοι, in fact, yet he is famous for his bride, who is herself imaginable as a πῶλος. The prevalence of the horse-breaking metaphor, therefore, allows this lyric to humorously recast the Homeric epithet κλυτόπωλος so that it does not mean "of famous foals" but rather "of *the* famous foal," that is, Persephone.

Another fine example of the use of hippomorphic imagery in depicting sexually attractive women is furnished by Semonides, in his well-known iambic catalogue poem. He compares women to different sorts of animals, or rather states that different sorts of women descend from different sorts of animals, although there are two women who do not descend from animals, but from the sea and the earth, respectively. The various women are all said to descend from something whose characteristics can be observed in the woman herself: the shameless woman descends from a dog (12–20), the fickle woman descends from the sea (27–42), and the reluctantly hardworking woman descends from a donkey (43–49). The most beautiful, yet least helpful, woman comes from a horse:

τὴν δ' ἵππος ἁβρὴ χαιτέεσσ' ἐγείνατο,
ἣ δούλι' ἔργα καὶ δύην περιτρέπει,
κοὔτ' ἂν μύλης ψαύσειεν, οὔτε κόσκινον
ἄρειεν, οὔτε κόπρον ἐξ οἴκου βάλοι,
οὔτε πρὸς ἰπνὸν ἀσβόλην ἀλμένη
ἵζοιτ'. ἀνάγκηι δ' ἄνδρα ποιεῖται φίλον·
λοῦται δὲ πάσης ἡμέρης ἄπο ῥύπον
δίς, ἄλλοτε τρίς, καὶ μύροις ἀλείφεται,
αἰεὶ δὲ χαίτην ἐκτενισμένην φορεῖ
βαθεῖαν, ἀνθέμοισιν ἐσκιασμένην.
καλὸν μὲν ὦν θέημα τοιαύτη γυνὴ
ἄλλοισι, τῶι δ' ἔχοντι γίνεται κακόν

---

[19] Περὶ Ἱππικῆς, 2.1.

The delicate long-maned mare begat this woman, who turns away from slavish tasks and toil. She would not touch a mill nor lift a sieve. She wouldn't throw the shit out of the house nor sit near the oven for fear of soot. She makes her man familiar with necessity. She washes herself two or three times a day and anoints herself with perfumes. She constantly keeps her thick hair brushed out and shaded with flowers. Such a woman is a beautiful sight to other men, but brings evil for the man who has her.

Semonides 57–68

The point here is the stereotyping of the beautiful woman as useless, and thus less desirable than she may initially seem. As Egoscozábal points out, a significant contributing factor in the logic of the horse representing this woman lies in the role that horses played in large parts of ancient Greece: they were symbols of wealth and affluence, but did not actually do much labor.[20] The horse is presumably also fit for contrasting this woman with the woman who descends from a donkey, who is said to do all of her work, albeit grudgingly (43–45). Additionally, Gregory has shown that comparisons of horses and donkeys in ancient Greek are frequently coded as discussions of social and economic hierarchy.[21] So the use of a mare here may function to denigrate wealthy women, in order to suggest to the listener, who may not be able to marry a rich woman, that he is better off without one.[22]

The beauty of the horse is equally important, as the emphasis on her vanity here proves. The beauty of the woman is as recognizable in this mare as the salient qualities of the other women were in the sea and the donkey. It is worth noting that the narrator's description of the beautiful woman's similarity with the beauty of the horse focuses consistently on the mare's hair. Egoscozábal also points out that there is an element of reality in this depiction, since the maintenance of a horse requires that a great deal of care be dedicated to its hair.[23] I think that it is also important that the horses' hair is distributed much like that of humans, particularly in women, who are less likely to go bald, so this is an especially logical point of comparison. The focus on the hair of the horse/woman is an important element of the hippomorphizing and concomitant anthropomorphizing.[24] Its significance will be discussed at greater length shortly. Women

---

[20] Egoscozábal 2003:17. See also Aristophanes *Clouds* 1–87.
[21] Gregory 2007.
[22] See Griffith 2006:311–312 on the economic associations of hair, both human and equine.
[23] Egoscozábal 2003:17.
[24] See Griffith 2006:314–317 for further examples of the way that equine hair is imagined as reflecting human.

then, especially beautiful and young women, are easily compared to horses in Greek lyric because of their beauty and because of the connotations of breaking and taming in descriptions of horses, especially young ones.

In addition to literary comparisons of women to horses, Greece actually provides a wonderful example of literal female hippomorphism in the myth of the rape of Demeter by Poseidon. Although it is Poseidon who bore the title Hippios, and to whom horses were sacrificed, it was Demeter who was worshiped in hippomorphic form. Pausanias tells us that during his tour of Arcadia Demeter was still worshiped in the cave in which she was supposed to have taken refuge after the attack. The cult image of the goddess which was set up there is described thus:

> ἄγαλμα ἀναθεῖναι ξύλου. πεποιῆσθαι δὲ οὕτω σφίσι τὸ ἄγαλμα·
> καθέζεσθαι μὲν ἐπὶ πέτρᾳ, γυναικὶ δὲ ἐοικέναι τἄλλα πλὴν κεφαλήν·
> κεφαλὴν δὲ καὶ κόμην εἶχεν ἵππου.

> They dedicated a statue of wood. They made it thus: it sat on a rock, and resembled a woman except for the head. It had the head and hair of a horse.

> Pausanias VIII 42.3–4

We see sex, hippomorphism, and male power linked even more clearly and explicitly than in the literary passages, but this same assemblage of themes can be documented throughout these texts, and they are the same themes that are joined in the PIE horse sacrifice.

To return to that horse sacrifice, then, it was seen there that the principal unifying theme of the various descendant traditions was an overlap of human and equine identity, exemplified in hippomorphism. Furthermore it was clear that the parent culture found this ontological coincidence to be especially useful in thinking about sex and demonstrated a nexus whereby hippomorphic sex was symbolically linked to expressions of male power and authority. This nexus of ideas is culturally unique, and the fact that the exact same nexus exists in Greece means that its presence there is best understood as one of inheritance, not of coincidence. To be clear, what I am suggesting is not that erotically tinged depictions of horses originate in the PIE horse sacrifice but simply that the parent culture used horses and their connection to humans as a means for thinking about sex and power and that the Greeks inherited elements of this tendency, as expressed in depictions both of women and of men, as we will now see.

Men and Horses

Despite the apparent ease with which the Semonides poem asserts the relationship between horses and female sexual attractiveness, this phenomenon is not entirely restricted to women, or to mares, as this passage by Ibycus readily documents:

Ἔρος αὖτέ με κυανέοισιν ὑπὸ
βλεφάροις τακέρ' ὄμμασι δερκόμενος
κηλήμασι παντοδαποῖς ἐς ἄπει-
ρα δίκτυα Κύπριδος ἐσβάλλει·
ἦ μὰν τρομέω νιν ἐπερχόμενον,
ὥστε φερέζυγος ἵππος ἀεθλοφόρος ποτὶ γήραι
ἀέκων σὺν ὄχεσφι θοοῖς ἐς ἅμιλλαν ἔβα.

Eros, glancing tenderly at me again from beneath his dark brows, with all sorts of enticements casts me into the inescapable nets of Aphrodite. Indeed I tremble at his approach, like a once prize-winning race horse now beset with old age that unwillingly goes to the track with the swift chariots.

Ibycus 287

In this case the man is apparently aging and presumably not as attractive as he once was, so he is merely an old stallion. Yet his earlier beauty is vouchsafed by his status as an ἀεθλοφόρος, "prize-winning," horse. This work imports the symbology of epic with its equation of the horse and hero, thereby activating the metaphor of courtship as competition, and hence war, so conventional in amatory poetry. It is important to note that we cannot know the gender of the love-object here and the erotic hippomorphism is articulated in terms not of sexual subjugation but of sexual agency: the lover is the horse, not the beloved. The narrator races with other men in pursuit of a common erotic object. There is still a differential of power operative here, certainly, but it works along a different axis. The horse is controlled not by a lover, as the Thracian girl by the ἱπποπείρης ἐμβάτης, but by Eros and Aphrodite. By casting himself as a horse the narrator engages in a pretense of powerlessness and reluctance by exploiting the relationship between horses, sexuality, and dominance, which, as the πῶλοι of Anacreon make clear, is integral to hippomorphic representations of humans.

Ibycus also reveals the latent erotic character of the comparison of epic heroes to horses. Although horses in the *Iliad* are primarily prized for their martial excellence, as are the men whom they aid in battle, physical beauty is conceived of in ancient Greece as attendant on other physical and moral excellence for men as well as women. Thus the Homeric heroes are not only brave, strong, and fast, but also exceptionally beautiful, as are their horses. For example, when Priam has come to terms with Achilles, the slayer of his son, the two men marvel at each other's physical beauty:

αὐτὰρ ἐπεὶ πόσιος καὶ ἐδητύος ἐξ ἔρον ἕντο,
ἤτοι Δαρδανίδης Πρίαμος θαύμαζ' Ἀχιλῆα
ὅσσος ἔην οἷός τε· θεοῖσι γὰρ ἄντα ἐῴκει·
αὐτὰρ ὃ Δαρδανίδην Πρίαμον θαύμαζεν Ἀχιλλεὺς
εἰσορόων ὄψίν τ' ἀγαθὴν καὶ μῦθον ἀκούων.
αὐτὰρ ἐπεὶ τάρπησαν ἐς ἀλλήλους ὁρόωντες,
τὸν πρότερος προσέειπε γέρων Πρίαμος θεοειδής·

But when they had had their fill of food and drink, then Priam the son of Dardanus marveled at Achilles, how tall he was, and how good-looking; for he appeared like a god. But Achilles was marveling at Priam the son of Dardanus, gazing at his handsome face and hearing his noble speech. But after they enjoyed looking at one another, god-like Priam, the old man, spoke first.

Iliad XXIV 628–634

In this moment of daring and noble humility, Priam, despite his age, is still beautiful, and Achilles is fittingly as handsome as he is heroic. Achilles' beauty may lie in the background in the Ibycus lyric, since it recalls a moment in book XXII of the *Iliad* when Achilles himself is likened to a horse:

Ὣς εἰπὼν προτὶ ἄστυ μέγα φρονέων ἐβεβήκει,
σευάμενος ὥς θ' ἵππος ἀεθλοφόρος σὺν ὄχεσφιν,
ὅς ῥά τε ῥεῖα θέῃσι τιταινόμενος πεδίοιο·
ὣς Ἀχιλεὺς λαιψηρὰ πόδας καὶ γούνατ' ἐνώμα.

Speaking thus, he <u>went</u> [ἐβεβήκει; cf. ἔβα in Ibycus, line 7] to the city in high spirits, rushing like a <u>prize-winning</u> horse with a <u>chariot</u>,[25] a horse easily rushing at full speed over the plain. Thus did Achilles nimbly deploy his feet and knees.

Iliad XXII 21–24

---

[25] ὄχεσφιν, here and in Ibycus, displays the instrumental plural case ending, -φι(ν), which had lost much of its semantic distinctness in Homer. It is used to express instrumental, locatival, and ablative functions in both the singular and the plural. Hence, I have translated it as singular in one instance and plural in another as seemed most befitting the context.

As discussed in Chapters 1 and 2, Achilles' epithets and his connection to his chariot team make clear his horse-like qualities, so this comparison is completely logical. The similarity between Achilles and his horses, as discussed thus far, has primarily involved the overlap in martial prowess and ontology, the fact that he, like his chariot-team, is partly mortal and partly divine. The erotic import of this similarity has not yet been addressed, nor, I admit, is it obvious here.

Yet one character, Paris, is especially noted for his physical beauty, and as such it is particularly fitting that his prideful displays are compared to the prancing of a stallion. As he returns to the battlefield after having sex with Helen, Paris is described thus:

Οὐδὲ Πάρις δήθυνεν ἐν ὑψηλοῖσι δόμοισιν,
ἀλλ' ὅ γ', ἐπεὶ κατέδυ κλυτὰ τεύχεα ποικίλα χαλκῷ,
σεύατ' ἔπειτ' ἀνὰ ἄστυ ποσὶ κραιπνοῖσι πεποιθώς.
ὡς δ' ὅτε τις στατὸς ἵππος ἀκοστήσας ἐπὶ φάτνῃ
δεσμὸν ἀπορρήξας θείῃ πεδίοιο κροαίνων
εἰωθὼς λούεσθαι ἐϋρρεῖος ποταμοῖο
κυδιόων· ὑψοῦ δὲ κάρη ἔχει, ἀμφὶ δὲ χαῖται
ὤμοις ἀΐσσονται· ὃ δ' ἀγλαΐηφι πεποιθὼς
ῥίμφά ἑ γοῦνα φέρει μετά τ' ἤθεα καὶ νομὸν ἵππων·
ὣς υἱὸς Πριάμοιο Πάρις κατὰ Περγάμου ἄκρης
τεύχεσι παμφαίνων ὥς τ' ἠλέκτωρ ἐβεβήκει

Nor did Paris delay long in the lofty halls, but when he had donned his glorious armor, ornate with bronze, he rushed through the city trusting to his quick feet, just as a stable horse having eaten his fill at the manger breaks free of his bonds and rushes stamping over the plain, accustomed to bathing in the fair-flowing river. He holds his head high and lets his mane run down his shoulders. Reveling in his splendor, quickly his knees bear him to the haunts and pasture of the horses [or perhaps mares]. Thus did Paris, the son of Priam, come down from high Pergamum gleaming in his arms like the bright beaming sun.

Iliad VI 503–513

The comparison certainly rests to some extent on shared martial capacity, as the emphasis on feet and legs indicates, but the dominant theme is one of splendor.

It should also be noted that the mane of the horse is a focal point for the comparison. The horse's mane is said to flow over its shoulders. Although horses' manes can do this, this description sounds much more appropriate to a human, as in the Archilochean fragment 25: ἔχουσα θαλλόν μυρσίνης ἐτέρπετο /

ῥοδῆς τε καλόν ἄνθος ἥ δέ οἱ κόμη / ὤμους κατεσκίαζε, "she delighted holding a sprig of myrtle and the beautiful rose blossom, while her hair overshadowed her shoulders."[26] It is as if the horse is being anthropomorphized as Paris is being hippomorphized and their hair is the shared axis of the mutual transformation.

The similarity between this and the likening of Achilles to a horse is clear and is remarked upon on by Kirk. [27] Compare the use of σεύατ'/σευάμενος (VI 505; XXII 22), ποσὶ/ πόδας (VI 505; XXII 24), πεδίοιο/πεδίοιο (VI 507; XXII 23), γοῦνα/γούνατ' (VI 511; XXII 24), and ἐβεβήκει/ἐβεβήκει (VI 513; XXII 21). The similarity between this comparison, the horse simile employed by Ibycus, and the simile of the race horses used in Alcman's *Partheneion* make clear that the metaphor of a racing/fighting horse is a ready erotic image for both men and women. I would note that Paris' sexual attractiveness is part of the point of the simile, but his sexual agency is not questioned.[28] The fuller comparison of Paris to a horse makes the erotic nature of such a comparison clear, and suggests that Achilles' beauty underlies his own comparison to a horse as much as his speed and strength. The overlap in vocabulary reflected here and in the Ibycus lyric highlights how extensively the iconography of racing and battle coincide in hippological erotic imagery as well as prevalence of that erotic imagery itself, even without the intentional activation of an erotic setting.

It should be noted that parts of these two similes are combined in book XV, in a description of Hector in lines 263–269. Lines 263–268 are the same as those used to describe Paris, while line 269 ends with the final words of the simile that described Achilles:

ὡς δ' ὅτε τις στατὸς ἵππος ἀκοστήσας ἐπὶ φάτνῃ
δεσμὸν ἀπορρήξας θείη πεδίοιο κροαίνων
εἰωθὼς λούεσθαι ἐϋρρεῖος ποταμοῖο
κυδιόων· ὑψοῦ δὲ κάρη ἔχει, ἀμφὶ δὲ χαῖται
ὤμοις ἀΐσσονται· ὃ δ' ἀγλαΐηφι πεποιθὼς
ῥίμφά ἑ γοῦνα φέρει μετά τ' ἤθεα καὶ νομὸν ἵππων·
ὡς Ἕκτωρ λαιψηρὰ πόδας καὶ γούνατ' ἐνώμα

... just as a stable horse having eaten his fill at the manger breaks free of his bonds and rushes stamping over the plain, accustomed to bathing in the fair-flowing river. He holds his head high and lets his mane run down his shoulders. Reveling in his splendor, quickly his knees bear

---

[26] The flowers and hair here reflect jointly on womanhood here just as in Semonides.

[27] Kirk 1990:226–7.

[28] See Griffith 2006:313.

him to the haunts and pasture of the horses [or perhaps mares]. Thus did Hector nimbly deploy his feet and knees.

Iliad XV 263–269

Although Homeric vocabulary and formulas are often repeated, full similes rarely occur more than once.[29] Accordingly, Aristarchus athetized most of this simile (lines 265–268).[30] Janko, however, defends the authenticity of the simile by reminding us that Hector is also returning to battle and has good reason to exult.[31] Hector is, of course, beautiful himself, and although the context of the simile is less explicitly erotic when it is used of Hector than when it is used of Paris, the attractiveness of a hero is virtually inseparable from his martial prowess, so it is still sensible here, as well as in book VI.

The reference to Paris' hair in XV 266–267 is especially noteworthy since it recalls the depictions of hair seen in previous passages that dealt with women. Hair is, in fact, a frequent and almost universal focus of hippomorphizing passages. In Alcman's *Partheneion* it was the hair of the girl that demonstrated her superiority over her competition, at the very moment that she was compared to a beautiful horse:

ἦ οὐχ ὁρῃς; ὁ μὲν κέλης
Ἐνητικός· ἁ δὲ χαίτα
τᾶς ἐμᾶς ἀνεψιᾶς
Ἁγησιχόρας ἐπανθεῖ
χρυσὸς [ὡ]ς ἀκήρατος·

Don't you see? The courser is Venetic, but my cousin Hegesichora's hair blooms like unmixed gold.

Alcman *Partheneion* 50–54

The woman in Semonides' iambic poem was not like any mare but a long-maned mare (χαιτέεσσα, 57), and her self-absorbing beauty was typified by the fact that she constantly brushed and decorated her hair with flowers (αἰεὶ δὲ χαίτην ἐκτενισμένην φορεῖ | βαθεῖαν, ἀνθέμοισιν ἐσκιασμένην, 65–66).

---

[29] Moulton 1977:94.

[30] See Janko 1994:256.

[31] Janko also points out that similes often mark the opening of battle scenes and that equine similes are typical of this use (1994:256). In the *Iliad*, however, there are only these three equine similes, and although this is true of the simile involving Hector and the simile involving Achilles, it is not quite as true of the simile involving Paris. Although a battle does follow this simile, it is not a battle in which Paris features prominently.

The importance of the horse's hair as the focal point of hippomorphic comparisons can be seen nowhere more clearly than in the story of Pelopidas, discussed in Chapter 2 for its significance in regard to human sacrifice and the ease with which human sacrifice becomes or resembles horse sacrifice. I requote it here for convenience:

Ὁ δὲ Πελοπίδας ἐν τῷ στρατοπέδῳ κατακοιμηθεὶς ἔδοξε τάς τε παῖδας ὁρᾶν περὶ τὰ μνήματα θρηνούσας καὶ καταρωμένας τοῖς Σπαρτιάταις, τόν τε Σκέδασον κελεύοντα ταῖς κόραις σφαγιάσαι παρθένον ξανθήν, εἰ βούλοιτο τῶν πολεμίων ἐπικρατῆσαι ... πῶλος ἐξ ἀγέλης ἀποφυγοῦσα καὶ φερομένη διὰ τῶν ὅπλων, ὡς ἦν θέουσα κατ᾽ αὐτοὺς ἐκείνους, ἐπέστη· καὶ τοῖς μὲν ἄλλοις θέαν παρεῖχεν ἥ τε χρόα στίλβουσα τῆς χαίτης πυρσότατον, ἥ τε γαυρότης καὶ τὸ σοβαρὸν καὶ τεθαρρηκὸς τῆς φωνῆς· Θεόκριτος δ᾽ ὁ μάντις συμφρονήσας ἀνεβόησε πρὸς τὸν Πελοπίδαν· ἥκει σοι τὸ ἱερεῖον ὦ δαιμόνιε, καὶ παρθένον ἄλλην μὴ περιμένωμεν, ἀλλὰ χρῶ δεξάμενος ἣν ὁ θεὸς δίδωσιν.

When Pelopidas lay down to sleep in the camp he seemed to behold these girls weeping over their tombs and cursing the Spartans. He also saw Skedasos, their father, commanding him to sacrifice to the girls a red-haired maiden, if he desired victory over his enemies ... a filly broke away from a herd of horses and ran through the camp, and when it had run right up to them, it stood still. While the rest of the men were admiring the shining fiery color of her mane, and her exultant nature, as well as the vehemence and boldness of her voice, Theokritos, the seer, reflected and cried out to Pelopidas, "Your sacrifice has come, sir. Let us not wait for another maiden, but accept and use the one that the gods offer."

Plutarch *Life of Pelopidas* 21–22

It is the similarity in hair that confirms that this mare can be a ritual substitute for the girl: a red-haired mare can apparently be sacrificed in the place of a red-haired girl. This story also is not without sexual implications. The young women who were avenged in the defeat of the Spartans were the victims of sexual assault. The sacrificing of another young woman to them, or a young mare that can stand in for such a young woman, is evidently motivated by a desire for a sacrificial victim that reflects the identity of these Leuktridai, whose identity in this context is bound up in their position as sexual object. Note that the youth of the girls is made quite explicit: they are referred to as παῖδας, children, and κόραις, girls, and the horse that is sacrificed for them is a πῶλος, a word which imparts the notion of sexual inexperience and reluctance when used in application to humans. This sacrifice, the depictions of Paris returning to battle, Alcman's chorus, and Semonides' extravagant woman, all have roots in the equine capacity for near-human identity, as well as the symbolic utility of horses in reflecting human sexual attractiveness, which is frequently expressed through the similarity of horse and human hair.[32]

As a final example of the applicability of equine erotic imagery to depictions of both male and female sexual attractiveness, I would point to the use of a neuter form of ἵππος, τὸ ἵππον. Hesychius states that τὸ ἵππον could be used to refer to the sexual organs of males as well as females: τὸ μόριον καὶ τὸ τῆς γυναικὸς καὶ τοῦ ἀνδρός.[33] In relation to this, Egoscozábal cites numerous ancient authorities for the belief that both male and female horses were especially amorous animals.[34] Clearly the erotic signification of horses includes both males and females, even if erotic images of horses still conform to a dichotomy of gender representation. Just as we saw in Chapter 2 that martial similarities reflect inherited thought patterns, so too do erotic echoings.

It is of course true that use of hippological erotic imagery is not entirely confined to the world of ancient Greek literature, and slang term terms such as "stallion" and "filly" are common enough even in recent English parlance. There are hippological phrases for actual sexual acts in English as well. One only has to reflect upon the tenacity of the rumors about the proclivities of Catherine the Great to recognize that the association between horses and human sexuality has some currency, yet I know of no culture in which the tendency is quite so pronounced or quite so consistent with the PIE model as the early Greek. A tradition that is as long-lived as the one that I am postulating in the case of horses and sexuality would not be very plausible if were not also logical, and even if something very similar to this phenomenon occurs elsewhere, it is unlikely that all of the behaviors that the phenomenon demonstrates in ancient Greece

---

[32] This concept is not, perhaps, entirely lost in modern society. In the mid 1990s it was fashionable for young women to use horse shampoo to wash their hair. The children's toys sold under the name "My Little Pony" exploit the similarity between human and equine hair quite consistently. These hippomorphic dolls, which are produced in commercially feminizing color schemes, have long, full manes and are sold with brushes. These brushes, however, are oversized and the ad campaigns which promote the dolls encourage the children who own these dolls to brush their own hair with the brushes as well as the hair of the hippomorphic toy. The toys essentially function as avatars for the child and the communicating of identity is localized in the hair. See Rutherford 2007. The Indian horse sacrifice, incidentally, involves special care paid to the preparation of the horse's hair, which is adorned for the ceremony, but I know of no parallel treatment of the hair of the king.

[33] Latte 1996:372.

[34] Egoscozábal 2003:19.

occur elsewhere in precisely the same form. Additionally, the fact that such an association *can* occur in multiple cultures independently does not mean that it cannot be inherited as well. If the phenomenon can be identified in the culture of the PIE speakers and in ancient Greece, then the fact that the phenomenon is sensible or logical makes it all the more likely that it was operative in the intervening stages between the culture of the PIE speakers and that of the ancient Greeks and so represents a genuine inheritance.

Men-, Men, and Μένος— The Origins of the Metapoetic Charioteer

One facet of the erotic equine imagery that presents unique challenges to comparatists is the figure of the charioteer, because of the difficulty of identifying physical evidence of chariots in the parent culture. Although Greek chariots are deployed in erotic lyric, their treatment is one that grows quite naturally out of the inherent erotic function of the horse. Anacreon 417, already discussed, makes clear how easily sexual hierarchies are mapped onto human-horse relationships, and how the lover may be positioned as rider and horse-breaker. Anacreon 360, however, presents a horse that is not ridden but driven and the object of desire is positioned as the charioteer:

ὦ παῖ παρθένιον βλέπων
δίζημαί σε, σὺ δ' οὐ κοεῖς,
οὐκ εἰδὼς ὅτι τῆς ἐμῆς
ψυχῆς ἡνιοχεύεις.

Oh boy with the girlish glances, I'm pursuing you but you don't even notice, not knowing that you are the charioteer of my soul.

Anacreon 360

Comparable examples also occur elsewhere:

οὐδ' οἵδ' αἰνὸν ἔρωτος ἀπεστρέψαντο κυδοιμὸν
μαινομένου, δεινὸν δ' ἦλθον ὑφ' ἡνίοχον.

Nor did they escape the dreadful battle noise of raging Eros, but came under the terrible charioteer.

Hermesianax 7.83–84

οὔτ' ἀθείαστον ὁ τῶν ἐρώντων ἐνθουσιασμός ἐστιν οὔτ' ἄλλον ἔχει
θεὸν ἐπιστάτην καὶ ἡνίοχον ἢ τοῦτον, ᾧ νῦν ἑορτάζομεν καὶ θύομεν.

The enthusiasm of lovers is not without divine inspiration and has no
other god as driver and charioteer than that one for whom we now
celebrate and offer sacrifice.

Plutarch *Amatorius* 759D5

A particularly interesting extension of this metaphor is the Athenian marriage
ritual, in which the best-man is known as the πάροχος, the companion of a
chariot rider:

πάροχος καλεῖται διὰ τὸ μόνος αὐτὸς συναναβαίνειν καὶ ὀχουμένῳ τῷ
νυμφίῳ παροχεῖσθαι.

He is called the πάροχος because he mounts the chariot and is carried
along with the groom.[35]

Eustathius *Commentarii ad Homeri Iliadem* II 351.6–7

Although our data are limited, it seems perhaps that while women are depicted
as horses, men may be depicted as horses or charioteers. In any case, the
inherent connections between horses and sex seen elsewhere make this particular development quite natural.

What is particularly exciting here is that recognition of the deep connection between horses and poetic depictions of human sexuality in Greece and the
further IE world may provide a key to understanding one of the most fascinating
figures in Greek poetry, the metapoetic charioteer. The depiction of poetry as a
chariot in Greece is relatively common, especially in Pindar. For example:

ὦ Φίντις, ἀλλὰ ζεῦξον ἤδη
μοι σθένος ἡμιόνων,
ᾇ τάχος, ὄφρα κελεύθῳ τ' ἐν καθαρᾷ
βάσομεν ὄκχον, ἵκωμαί τε πρὸς ἀνδρῶν
καὶ γένος·

But Phintis, come now yoke for me the strength of the mules, quickly, so
that I may mount the chariot on a clean path and arrive at the lineage
of the heroes.

Olympian VI 22–25

[35] Latte 1966:718.

The method by which he comes to and details the lineage of heroes is, of course, his song, and that song is here a chariot. He concludes *Olympian* I

γλυκυτέραν κεν ἔλπομαι
σὺν ἅρματι θοῷ κλεΐ-
ξειν ἐπίκουρον εὑρὼν ὁδὸν λόγων

I hope to celebrate a sweeter [victory] still, with the swift chariot, finding the helpful path of words.

Olympian I 109–110

Here, just as in *Olympian* VI, the metaphor of the chariot of song is combined with the metaphor of the path of song, an image that may also be of IE or Greco-Indo-Iranian origin. In *Isthmian* VIII we are told that the chariot of the Muses is rushing ahead to celebrate the memory of Nikokles the boxer.

ἔσ-
συταί τε Μοισαῖον ἅρμα Νικοκλέος
μνᾶμα

And the chariot of the Muses rushes to the memory of Nikokles

Isthmian VIII 61–62

Olympian IX and *Pythian* X have similar images:

εἴην εὑρησιεπὴς ἀναγεῖσθαι
πρόσφορος ἐν Μοισᾶν δίφρῳ

I wish to be a finder of words as I move forward as gift bearer in the Muses' chariot.

Olympian IX 80–81

τόδ' ἔζευξεν ἅρμα Πιερίδων τετράορον

yoked this four-horse chariot of the Muses.

Pythian X 65

Non-Pindaric instances exist as well, of course. Parmenides is also an obvious example, from outside of epinician poetry. The Greek applications of this metaphor are rather diverse in fact, but its origins are pre-Greek.

This is clear because the metaphor is quite common in early Iranian and Indian poetry, two of the earliest literatures from cultures that share a common ancestor with the Greek. Our earliest poetic texts from Iran are the Gathas. Composed perhaps as early as 1000 BCE, the Gathas represent a very small assortment of hymns written in the Old Avestan language and embedded in broader Zoroastrian liturgy, which is generally written in a later form of the language. In these hymns the words of the poet, Zarathustra, are imagined as proceeding from the poet's mouth upwards to heaven in the form of a chariot. They are, in fact, occasionally imagined as engaged in a great chariot race, competing with the hymns of other singers, in a competition to reach heaven and achieve fulfillment. For example the poet asks

> hizuuō raiθim
> mahiiā rāzəng vahū sāhīt mananghā

> May the giver of intellect instruct with good thought the chariot horse of my tongue.

> *Yasna* 50.6

Also the singer proclaims his talent by asserting

> vaēda xuaraiθiiā vaintiia srauua

> I know victorious songs conducted by their own charioteer.

> *Yasna* 28.10

In predicting the culmination of his prayer he says that

> at asištā yaojante ā hušitōiš vanghəuš mananghō
> mazdā ašaxiiācā yōi zazənti vanghāu srauuahī

> The swiftest horses will be yoked for a race to the dwelling of good thought, and of Mazda, and of Truth, those which will win good fame

> *Yasna* 30.10

Good fame is that which is attained through song. The search for fame then is expressed as a chariot race of songs. In this regard it is not unlike the epinicians of Pindar. In both cases the song is imagined as a chariot.

The image of the song as chariot and the singer as charioteer is also common enough in the *Ṛgveda*, the earliest layer of Indian poetry.[36] In the description of the invention of sacrificial ritual (10.130), we are told that the Gayatri meter (a

---

[36] A survey of the general deployments of chariot based imagery in the Vedas, including metapoetic deployments, can be found in Sparreboom 1985:13–27.

common hymnic meter) is the yoke-mate of Agni, imagined as a horse. In hymn 1.61 to Indra the singer says

stomaṃ saṃ hinomi rathaṃ na taṣṭeva

with my tongue, I set in motion my hymn, as would a fashioner of a chariot

Ṛgveda I.61.5

In hymn 5.73, to the Aśvins, the horse men, the poet says

yā takṣāma rathāṃ ivāvocāma bṛhan namaḥ

Which we have fashioned as a chariot. We have proclaimed great virtue.

Ṛgveda V.73.10

There are other examples as well, but these few will suffice here to document the existence of the phenomenon.[37] This was then a particular metaphorical tradition inherited commonly by the Greeks, Indians, and Iranians from a common parent that routinely linked not only heroes and patrons with equestrian excellence, but also poets themselves.

Current archaeological evidence, however, does not permit the conclusion that horses were used in the drawing of these wagons, since no harness suitable for horses, rather than oxen, is known to have been invented before 2500 BCE, well after the breakup of the PIE speakers, however that event is to be understood or dated.[38] It is probable, then, that the domesticated horse was kept by the PIE speakers as a food and as a riding animal without being put into the harness. So domesticated horses existed and wagons existed before the IE diaspora, but horses were not put to wagons until afterward, a development that must have happened independently in each culture.

It seems unlikely then that the metapoetic charioteer is an inherited feature after all. So where does it comes from? I think that the similarity in treatment across these languages is too consistent to be coincidence. I suggest simply that the origins of the metaphor have less to do with charioteers themselves than with the domesticated horse and with the symbology of that horse in IE culture.[39] I suggest that a common equine ideology was inherited in all three

---

[37] Several examples of this phenomenon are also discussed by West (2007:42–43).

[38] See Introduction, pages 4–5.

[39] It is, of course, possible that new archaeological evidence will emerge and the date of this development will be pushed back so far that it may be seen a common inheritance after all. Even if

cultures and then developed along parallel lines in the three cultures. There are some reasons for this that are obvious. The aristocratic world to which much of this poetry belonged may well have been the same world to which horses belonged, in both Greek and pre-Greek times. If horses were a symbol of wealth and of heroic martial virtue in early Indo-European times, as they probably were, then they would have been easily adopted by poets wishing to address those themes and situate their own work within that world.

There are perhaps less obvious reasons as well and one of them, I suggest, has its roots in the connection between horses and sex. I speak here of a particular sort of force embodied by the horse, a force that itself had special connections to horses and to poetry. What I mean by this is an extension of an idea described by Max Latona in his article comparing Parmenides to one of the Indian Upanishads.[40] He points out that when early IE poets describe the curbing of passions they often describe it in ways that are hippological. In Homer, in fact, the checking of one's own strong internal desires is often described as "taming, checking, and bridling," all hippological vocabulary in which the human's emotional and psychological forces are likened to the physical force of the horse.[41] There was then, even in early IE times, a traditional metaphor linking horses and human emotional forces. This emotional force is, however, also an intellectual and poetic force and is signaled by one of the Homeric horse's most salient and, I think, characteristic possessions, that is, its μένος. Μένος is, of course, associated with Homeric heroes themselves but is also regularly possessed by and placed in horses:

Ὣς εἰπὼν ἵπποισιν ἐνέπνευσεν μένος ἠΰ.

So speaking he breathed great μένος into the horses

Iliad XVII 456

τίς γάρ τοι Ἀχαιῶν ἄλλος ὁμοῖος
ἵππων ἀθανάτων ἐχέμεν δμῆσίν τε μένος τε

But who else among the Achaeans is of such kind as to hold mastery over and check the μένος of the immortal horses.[42]

Iliad XVII 475–476

---

this were to happen, however, the inheritance of ideology and imagery described here would not cease to be meaningful.

[40] Latona 2008.
[41] Latona 2008:224.
[42] My translation is influenced by Edwards 1991:110.

ἐν γὰρ Ἀθήνη
ἵπποις ἧκε μένος καὶ ἐπ' αὐτῷ κῦδος ἔθηκε.

For Athena sent μένος into his horses and gave glory to him.

Iliad XXIII 399–400

In Indo-Iranian poetry the connection is more varied but clearly present. In the Ṛgveda horses are said to have been formed from the cognate term *manas* (I.120.2), by the craftsman gods. They are often compared to the intellectual power of *manas*, being swifter than *manas* (*manaso javīya*),[43] and yoked to *manas* (*manoyuja*).[44] Poetic connotations are especially clear here as songs are also said to be *manoyuja*.[45] Chariots are also yoked to *manas*.[46] *Manas* here indicates the intellectual and creative force of the poet, but it is expressed through a metaphorical language in which horses are that *manas*.

This term belongs to one of the more fleshed out of the IE etymological networks. It is itself very simple, an e-grade s-stem noun derived from the verbal root *men-. The root is usually defined as something like "to think," but its derivatives have a surprisingly wide range of meanings.[47] To begin with there is the item currently under discussion, *menos*, with perfect cognates in Sanskrit *manas* and Avestan *manah*, displaying meanings ranging from "strength," to "mind," to "spirit." Some derivatives also have emotional import, such as δυσμενής, "hostile," which has perfect cognates in the Sanskrit *durmanas* and Avestan *dušmanah*. Several derivatives also have to do with anger, such as μῆνις, "rage," and μενεαίνω, to "rage."[48] Perhaps the most famous are the words having to do with memory and, in the world of oral poetry, with the production of poetry. The function of this root in regard to Greek conceptions of poetic production is typified in the word μιμνήσκω and the muse Μνεμοσύνη.[49]

The connotation that is least discussed, however, is the sexual. In Greek the wooer of a bride is a μνηστήρ, and the verbal expression of his activity is μνάομαι, which can also mean "to think." More bluntly, μένος can also mean semen, as proven by the Cologne Archilochus.[50] The sexual connotations of this

---

[43] Ṛgveda IX.97.28; of the chariot drawn by the horses and, therefore, the horses themselves Ṛgveda I.117.2, I.118.1, I.181.3, I.183.1, X.39.12, X.112.2.

[44] Ṛgveda I.14.6, I.51.10, IV.48.4.

[45] Ṛgveda VIII.13.26, IX.100.3.

[46] Ṛgveda VIII.5.2.

[47] Rix defines it as "*einen Gedanken fassen*" (2001:435), Pokorny as "*denken*" (1959:725), and Meillet as *mentem moueri* (1897:10).

[48] On the etymology of μῆνις see Muellner 1996:177–194.

[49] Martin 1989:78–79.

[50] ἀφῆκα μένος, ξανθῆς ἐπιψαύ[ων τριχός]. See Sickle 1975.

root, incidentally, were suggested by Gregory Nagy in his work on Greek and Indic meter.[51] Sexuality and semen are things to which the IE horse is often connected, as they are a surprisingly prominent elements of equine mythology.[52] Semen is an important feature of the mythology of the Aśvins and, as discussed in Chapter 2, a horse is even said to have sprung from the spilled semen of Poseidon. Moreover, the Vedas give stallions the unusual epithet *retodhā*, "semen-giver," for their role in the *aśvamedha*.[53]

The root *men-, then, deals with thought, emotion, memory, and sex. Perhaps then it should not be translated as "to think" but rather as "to direct one's life force," or something similar. The direction of this force could result in a sexual and reproductive act, a valorous act, or even an intellectual and poetic act. I suggest that the horse may have embodied the force expressed by this root, even in early IE times. This would not be surprising considering the unique function of the horse in early IE society, both practically and sacrificially. Given the associations of such a force it would not be hard to imagine that it played a significant part in the development of this metapoetic image.

The PIE horse sacrifice helps to show that Greece was the inheritor of an ideology that uniquely linked horses and humans, and that made use of horses to think about sex and power. This inherited ideology exerted influence over depictions of sacrifice, as seen in Chapter 2, but also seems to have colored Greek erotic depictions of humans generally, both male and female. The linkage between sex and horses, preserved in the ritual, also helps to explain the image of the metaphor of the metapoetic charioteer, common in Greece, India, and in Iran, since the horse seems to have had a special connection to μένος and the PIE verbal root *men-, to which poets also have a special connection. This root and its derivative μένος encapsulate an ancient concept of life force that expressed itself in both poetic acts and sexual acts.

---

[51] Nagy 1974:265.
[52] Doniger O'Flaherty 1980:174–175, 184.
[53] Vājasaneyi-Saṃhitā XXIII.20.

4

Chariots and the Ἵππιος Νόμος

THE METAPOETIC CHARIOTEER introduced at the end of the last chapter is but one example of the sort of similarity in the treatment of chariots and charioteers that one is likely to find among the IE cultures. When faced with such correspondences the reader may find it difficult to accept the archaeological conclusion that chariots are not themselves a common inheritance.[1] Yet it must be true that cultures linked by common heritage can develop in similar ways at least in isolated circumstances, and I think that alternative etymologies for these sorts of cultural overlaps can usually be found if one looks to what we do know was inherited. In the case of the metapoetic charioteer found in India, Greece, and Iran, we saw that its origin can be found not in the chariot itself, but in the symbolism of the horses to which the chariot is attached. The symbology of the horse will not, however, always be the inherited feature that best explains the parallel treatment of chariots in daughter cultures, and we must be prepared to search widely for answers to this sort of problem. The final subject of this study, therefore, is the use of chariots in bridal contests in Greek and Indic myths, a similarity that is best explained as a permutation of a mutually inherited marriage contest tradition.

The similarity that I refer to appears in the chariot races for Sūryā, the daughter of the sun, and for Hippodameia. The Indian divine horsemen, the Aśvins, share Sūryā as a common wife whom they seem to have married after winning a chariot race–based marriage contest that reminds readers of the chariot race of Pelops for Hippodameia, described in Pindar's self-styled ἵππιος

---

[1] I repeat that my argument here is based on what seems to be the best archaeological evidence that we have to date. If new evidence emerges, however, that requires the horse-drawn chariot to be viewed as a common IE inheritance then the arguments here will require modification. They will not, however, need to be disregarded. The poetic and ideological inheritance described here would simply need to be viewed as complimentary phenomena, informing the poetic depictions of that inherited technology.

νόμος, his horsey tune, *Olympian* I.[2] Details of the event are vague, but Jamison has shown convincingly that it was a contest, and the fact that it involved chariots is quite clear from the texts that we have, even if little else is:[3]

vīḷupatmabhirāśuhemabhirvā devānāṃ vā jūtibhiḥ śāśadānā |
tad rāsabho nāsatyā sahasramājā yamasya pradhane jighāya ||

Triumphing through your fast ones of strong wings or the incitements of the gods, O Nāsatyas [Aśvins], your donkey won a thousand in Yama's contest[4]

Ṛgveda I.116.2

rathamadyā daṃsiṣṭhamūtaye |
yamaśvinā suhavā rudravartanī ā sūryāyai tasthathuḥ ||

[I have called] for protection today that powerful chariot which the well-invoked Aśvins with rosy paths mounted for Sūryā

Ṛgveda VIII.22.1

It is safe to say that a chariot race was held for the right to marry Sūryā, even if there is no good description of the contest itself.[5] We have then two disparate IE traditions that each indicate the coming of suitors to compete in a chariot race for the right to marry a woman, and it is tempting to pursue a common mythic tradition here. I think that we should, but not one rooted in chariots.

As I stated earlier, my opinion is that the chariot need not itself be an inherited possession in two IE cultures for their similarities in chariot-based mythology to share common ancestry. I suggest that these traditions are cognate, and demonstrably so, regardless of the date of the invention of the

---

[2] ἐμὲ δὲ στεφανῶσαι | κεῖνον ἱππίῳ νόμῳ | Αἰοληΐδι μολπᾷ | χρή, "I must crown him with an Aeolian song, a horsey tune" (I 100–103). This designation must refer to the thoroughly equestrian nature of the ode, since it begins with a description of Hieron's horses, then proceeds to a chariot race, and ends with a metaphor of the poet as charioteer (discussed in Chapter 3).

[3] In his seminal work on Indian marriage contests Schmidt (1987:77–78) declined to accept this as an example thereof because, although it certainly resembles a contest, the intransparency of the source texts hindered him from that conclusion. Jamison has, however, shown that this must indeed be a contest myth (2001 and 2003). Her argument showcases how this particular treatment of chariot imagery grows out of Indian marriage rituals, and has even identified unique poetic formula treatment dealing with the verb root √vrā, 'to choose', that is special to depictions of marriage contests.

[4] Their chariot is usually yoked to magnificent horses, but it is occasionally said to have been yoked to a donkey. See Jhala 1978:78.

[5] For a fuller account of the passages that relate to this story and indicate the centrality of chariots to it see Pischel and Geldner 1889:14–30 and Jamison 2001.

chariot itself, because their relationship lies not in a chariot race myth per se, but rather in an inherited tradition of bridal contests of which each of these is an independently expectable outgrowth. The broad network of marriage contest myths documented in Greece and in India testify to a surprisingly consistent pattern of mythic variation, and the races of Pelops and of the Aśvins both partake in these patterns. One of the variations in these patterns is a chariot race, independently created in each culture but in each case indebted to the parent culture for the pattern of variation out of which it grew. They do not *have* to descend from a PIE chariot race myth in order to be cognate. They are more likely to be independently generated variants on an inherited model of bridal competition myth that has been melded to a local chariot race tradition. I propose then a dissection of Pindar's depiction of this race, and the idiosyncrasies therein, in the hope that when the patterns behind those idiosyncrasies are made evident the relationship of the two chariot myths will be visible. This analysis will begin with Pindar, then move on to related stories from India, after which I will propose a model for understanding their relationship. Once that model is established the relationship between these and the marriage of the Aśvins will become clear.

It is essential to note that Pindar's account of the victory of Pelops over Oinomaos for the right to marry Hippodameia in *Olympian* I contains several mythical idiosyncrasies.[6] The most dramatic involves the hymn's explicit rejection of cannibalism from the story of Tantalos (35ff.),[7] but there are several other examples as well: Poseidon's gift of horses to Pelops (75–87),[8] the winged nature of those horses (87),[9] and the absence of Oinomaos' charioteer Myrtilos, who helps rig the contest.[10] This last idiosyncrasy is the most important concern because there are uniquely relevant IE mythic comparanda which can shed light on the role of Myrtilos in this myth, and in so doing unpack the connections between a wide range of related myths. Consideration of these comparanda

---

[6]   Much of the ensuing analysis has appeared before, but with no account taken of the relationship of the Aśvins to this mythical complex or to the methodological lessons to be learned from the similarity of these two chariot race stories (Platte 2011). For general discussion of the Pindaric ode, including apparent mythological variation therein, see Gerber 1982 and Fisker 1990.

[7]   The text of *Olympian* I comes from Gerber 1982. The bibliography on this particular detail is quite large, but most scholars have concluded that Pindar's account is an innovation. See Köhnken 1974:200n3; Kakridis 1930. Cf. Nagy 1990b:116–135.

[8]   Köhnken 1974.

[9]   Gerber 1982:134–136. The horses were apparently winged on the Kypselos chest described by Pausanias (V 17.7) and appear as such on one black-figure vase (Göttingen University, J22, by the Sappho Painter). See Shapiro 1994:80–81.

[10]   We also find here the alternative punishment for Tantalos, in which he is not tempted with unattainable food, but rather a rock is perilously suspended over his head (54–64). See Gantz 1993:2.532.

makes it clear that *Olympian* I simply preserves one version of the myth, taken from a multiform mythic landscape whose origins are to be found in IE antiquity, and whose origins had significant influence on important scenes from Greek and Indian literature, some of which involve chariots.

Olympian I was composed for Hieron of Syracuse to celebrate a victory in the single horse race of 476 BCE, and Pelops' race against Oinomaos fittingly appears as the central myth of the hymn, which is the myth's earliest source.[11] Oinomaos established the race as a means of delaying his daughter's marriage,[12] and all of the previous challengers (of whom there were as many as seventeen)[13] had lost and been killed by Oinomaos. In the end, Pelops was victorious because of divine aid from Poseidon, at least in this account. Pindar relates that Pelops prayed to Poseidon for help, was given winged horses, and then won the race. Despite a lengthy prelude, Pindar's account of the race itself is remarkably brief:

> ... οὐδ' ἀκράντοις ἐφάψατο ἔπεσι. τὸν μὲν ἀγάλλων θεός
> ἔδωκεν δίφρον τε χρύσεον πτεροῖσίν τε ἀκάμαντας ἵππους.
> ἕλεν δ' Οἰνομάου βίαν παρθένον τε σύνευνον·

> He did not apply himself to fruitless words. Honoring him the god gave
> a golden chariot and horses untiring in wing. He overcame Oinomaos
> and took the maiden as bride.

Olympian I 86–88

Outside of this text, however, the victory is generally attributed to cheating.[14] Oinomaos' charioteer Myrtilos is usually reported to have rigged the race, at Hippodameia's request, by tampering with the axles.[15] Although it has

---

[11] This myth is fitting here because it is itself a chariot race, but also because the race and the resulting death of Oinomaos are linked to the founding of the Olympic games. Nagy 1990b: 117–120.

[12] According to some sources he believed that he would die if his daughter married (as, in fact, he did), while other sources suggest that he was in love with his daughter himself. Gantz 1993: 2.542–543.

[13] Gantz 1993:2.540.

[14] Our earliest source for cheating in this myth is Pherekydes (3 F 37a), but several others exist, for details of which see Gantz 1993:2.541–543. Among such sources are Apollonius, Apollodorus, and Hyginus. Myrtilos is also mentioned in Sophokles' *Elektra* (505–515) and in Euripides' *Orestes* (988–994). Both accounts depict his murder at the hands of Pelops. This occurred because Myrtilos attempted to instigate a sexual encounter with Hippodameia, which he believed he was owed for helping in the race. On the prevalence of Myrtilos and cheating in the artistic tradition see Lacroix 1976.

[15] Sometimes Pelops is said to have convinced Myrtilos to do this himself. The most common version asserts that Myrtilos replaced the axles with wax, but Pherecydes says that he did not insert the linchpin (Σ AR 1.752 = 3 F 37a).

been difficult to prove, most scholars have presumed that the Myrtilos episode predates Pindar's account, but that it was excluded from *Olympian* I to prevent any awkwardness in the comparison of Pelops' victory to Hieron's.[16] A comparison of related Greek myths with similar scenes from IE myth supports the belief that this element predates Pindar's account, but it points to a phenomenon that is much more complicated than one of simple omission. It points instead to a multiform mythic landscape predating Pindar's account, from which *Olympian* I preserves only one version.

One important strain of comparative evidence comes from later European folklore and has been discussed by Hansen.[17] He has already proposed that Pindar's account of the race reflects just one of multiple coexisting traditions,[18] and he illustrates this by incorporating into his analysis a rarely discussed version of the myth. This version, contained in Theopompos, indicates that Pelops buries his own charioteer, Killos, on the way to the contest for Hippodameia, after which the ghost of Killos helps him win the race. Hansen compares various versions of the myth with several later stories from medieval and Renaissance Europe which testify to a widely occurring folktale identified as the *Bride Won in a Tournament*.[19] This folktale describes a man who pays for a stranger's funeral, then travels to enter a tournament for the right to marry a woman. On the way he encounters the ghost of the buried man, who gives him horses and other resources for the tournament, which he wins. Hansen suggests that our Greek stories reflect coexisting traditions that contain elements of an earlier tale that corresponded to the *Bride Won in a Tournament*. This is a theory that I find illuminating, but I believe that it requires expansion due to other comparative evidence from ancient India, namely the epic tradition of the *svayaṃvara*.

In general, the *svayaṃvara*, or "self-choice" ceremony (*svayam*, "one's own"; *vara*, "choice"), involves the gathering of men to sue for the right to marry a particular woman, and I say that a corresponding tradition exists in the *svayaṃvaras* of epic poetry specifically, because they include the special feature of difficult challenges designed to determine the future husband.[20] The similarity between this and the contest for Hippodameia is obvious and the extent of overlap between the epic *svayaṃvaras* and choosing-ceremony legends in

---

[16] Gerber 1982:136; Köhnken 1974:203.

[17] Hansen 2000. Hansen also discusses this issue, in briefer form elsewhere (2002:56–62).

[18] Nagy has also suggested that the variant comes from a coexisting tradition rather than an innovative one (1990b:116–135).

[19] Hansen 2000:26.

[20] In addition to the epic *svayaṃvara*, known as the *vīryaśulka svayaṃvara*, Schmidt identifies two other distinct varieties in India (1987:76–109). The relationship of the contest for Hippodameia to Indian epic *svayaṃvaras* has been noted before, but, to my knowledge, the implications of this relationship for Pindar's particular account have not been elucidated. See Russo 2004:95.

Greece makes a genetic relationship between them difficult to deny. The story of Hippodameia then appears to share a genetic relationship with two other traditions, the epic *svayaṃvara* and the *Bride Won in a Tournament*. A comparison of all three traditions, however, presents such a complicated set of correspondences that it requires a broader investigation than has yet been attempted.

Although they do not involve chariots, the most famous of these choosing-ceremonies in India and Greece are those for Draupadī in the *Mahābhārata* and for Penelope in the *Odyssey*, and the similarities between them make an excellent place to start such an investigation.[21] The relevant plot of the *Mahābhārata* may be summarized as follows: two families, the Pāṇḍavas and the Kauravas, are in dispute over who should rule the kingdom of Kurukṣetra in northern India.[22] The Pāṇḍavas have the better claim, but are attacked and expelled by the Kauravas, after which they go into exile, disguised as Brahmins (wandering priests who beg for alms). In the course of this wandering they come to the city of King Drupada, where a choosing-ceremony is taking place for his daughter Draupadī. The king suspects that Arjuna, one of the exiled Pāṇḍavas, is in attendance and he decides to rig the contest in Arjuna's favor. Because Arjuna is famous as an archer, Drupada devises an archery-based contest to select the winner. He has a bow made so stiff that no else should be able to draw it and has an elaborate target suspended above the arena which the suitors must hit.[23] Although many other men fail in this task Arjuna succeeds, in disguise.[24]

The similarity of this contest to the one that occurs in book XXI of the *Odyssey* is clear. After the long absence of Odysseus, Penelope announces to her gathered suitors that she will remarry and that her future husband will have to complete a particular archery-based challenge. He will have to string a nearly unstringable bow and then use it to shoot an arrow through a series of axe heads.[25] After the others prove incapable, with the possible exception of Telemachus,[26] Odysseus, who has been disguised as a beggar, takes up the chal-

---

[21] Similarities between these two scenes, as well as some of the others that I will discuss, have been examined by Jamison (1999).

[22] For a fuller summary of the *Mahābhārata*, as well as a general introduction to its study see Brockington 1998.

[23] The relevant text is *Mahābhārata* I.175–179.

[24] One other man, Karṇa, does complete the task, but is rejected by Draupadī, ostensibly because of his lineage. Cf. Jamison 1999:246n49.

[25] The exact nature of the shot that Odysseus performs is difficult to determine, i.e. in exactly what way does an arrow move through axe heads: διὰ δ' ἀμπερὲς ἦλθε θύραζε | ἰὸς χαλκοβαρής (XXI 422–423)? See Russo 2004:95–97; Walcot 1984:357–369; Page 1973:95–113. The precise nature of the shot is, however, less important here than the general sort of contest to which it belongs.

[26] Telemachus begins to string the bow, and also seems likely to succeed, until his father signals him to stop (XXI 124–135).

lenge and succeeds. The parallels between these scenes are striking and could quickly lead one to reconstruct a PIE or Greco-Indo-Iranian choosing-ceremony myth, which involved a disguised hero, a bow, and a difficult target. I would, in fact, assume that choosing-ceremony tales of that type were told, but that they must have been only one variety.

India's other great epic, the *Rāmāyaṇa*, includes a choosing-ceremony that makes it difficult to maintain that these stories descend from a proto-myth in any simple fashion.[27] The *Rāmāyaṇa* is principally concerned with the abduction of Sītā and her husband Rāma's siege of the city of Laṅkā to retrieve her, but it also describes the choosing-ceremony that first leads to their marriage.[28] Here too suitors must string a nearly unstringable bow. Rāma does not in fact string it, but bends it so far that it actually snaps in half, which suffices, and afterward he marries Sītā. The similarities between this and the previous stories are as striking as are the differences. There is a bow that no one else can string, but there is no difficult target and there is no disguise. The similarities between these myths are too precise to dismiss, but we do not seem to be dealing with descent from one single story, but perhaps a similar series of thematically joined narratological conventions.

Two more relevant choosing-ceremonies from the *Mahābhārata*, both from the embedded story of Nala and Damayantī, help make this point clear.[29] This is a story told to the exiled Pāṇḍavas by a man who intends to prove to them that others have had fortune as bad as theirs. Accordingly it is a story of a man who lost his own kingdom and was forced into exile in a sort of disguise, just as they were. This man, Nala, was also separated from his wife, Damayantī, during his exile, although he is eventually reunited with her. He is also disguised, having been cursed so that he became unrecognizably short and deformed. Having abandoned his wife, he takes work as another man's charioteer. His wife Damayantī, however, obtains some knowledge of his whereabouts and devises a clever stratagem to entice him to return to her. She announces her own choosing-ceremony, ostensibly designed to find a new husband, but mentions it only in the presence of Nala's employer. She also schedules the event for the next morning. Nala is so skilled as a horseman that his ability to get there by the next morning would help testify to his identity. After Nala arrives the next morning for the choosing-ceremony, he and Damayantī are reunited.[30]

---

[27] On the *Rāmāyaṇa* in general, see Brockington 1998.

[28] The relevant text here is *Rāmāyaṇa* I.66.

[29] *Mahābhārata* III.52–79.

[30] Although this fact does not figure into my analysis, it may be interesting to note that Nala's chariot flies, as does that of Pelops.

Table 4.1. A Summary of Plot Elements from Other Choosing-Ceremonies

Draupadī	Penelope	Sītā	Damayantī (ii)[31]	Damayantī (i)
• marries Arjuna	• reunited with Odysseus	• marries Rāma	• reunited with Nala	• marries Nala
• bow contest winner	• bow contest winner	• bow contest	• chariot contest winner	• no contest
• disguised as Brahmin	• disguised as beggar	• no disguise	• disguised by curse	• everyone except winner disguised
• rigged by father	• rigged by Penelope?	• no rigging	• rigged by Damayantī	• rigged by Damayantī

Unlike the last three stories, this story has no bow, but it does contain the other elements that are common among the various myths.[32] It has disguise in the form of lower social rank, and in place of a bow that no one else can lift, it has chariot driving. The chariot driving is, I think, an example of the same contest motif exhibited by the other choosing-ceremony stories. Even if there is no official contest and no other competitors, the point of these contests is not really to find the best man, but to identify a man already chosen, just as happens here.

We also learn in this story how Nala and Damayantī were wed the first time, at another unusual choosing-ceremony. Damayantī knew of Nala beforehand and knew that she wanted to marry him. At the ceremony, however, she found that all of her suitors looked like Nala, because her other suitors were all gods who had chosen to thwart her attempt to pre-choose the groom by making it impossible for her to tell which was Nala. After much pleading from her they relented and allowed her to choose Nala. Unlike the other epic *svayaṃvaras* discussed here, this story does not actually have a contest at all. It has no special tasks, no weapons, but it does have disguise—a variation on the disguise motif that we have seen elsewhere, but disguise nonetheless.[33]

---

[31] These are listed in the order in which they appear in this discussion, not in the order in which they appear chronologically or even the order in which they appear in their texts. The reuniting of Nala and Damayantī, which I have discussed first, naturally follows their marriage in the text.

[32] Gresseth (1979) has discussed many of the similarities between the story of Nala and Damayantī and that of Odysseus and Penelope. He does not consider any other parallels but he nevertheless concludes that the contest of the bow was not a normal contest but rather a test to discover the pre-chosen suitor, Odysseus.

[33] This choosing-ceremony is discussed here because it features the disguise motif and because it involves preselection of the groom, but this is not actually a *vīryaśulka svayaṃvara* like the others. Jamison, following Schmidt, points out that this distinction is not absolute (1999:246).

The correspondences between these myths can be observed in Table 4.1, which is organized according to the woman for whom each contest is held. The motives of Penelope in setting up the bow contest are notoriously difficult to determine so they are designated as uncertain for the moment, although they will be discussed shortly.

Few of these stories involve precisely the same elements, but their constituent elements overlap enough to testify to a nexus of thematically related motifs, to a story-type that must be a common inheritance from a shared ancestor, most likely from the culture of the speakers of Proto-Indo-European, the ultimate parent language of both Greek and Sanskrit. This story-type seems to have featured a difficult feat, a piece of special equipment, the hero in disguise, and the manipulation of the contest on the hero's behalf, as may be inferred from Table 4.2, which integrates the information from the table above with the information from the Pindaric and non-Pindaric accounts of the contest for Hippodameia:

Table 4.2. Table of Narratological Correspondences

	Hippodameia (Pindaric)	Hippodameia (non-Pindaric)	Draupadī	Penelope	Sītā	Damayantī (ii)	Damayantī (i)
difficult feat	X	X	X	X	X	X	
special equipment	X	X	X	X	X	X	
disguise			X	X		X	X
contest rigged		X	X	?		X	X

Based solely on the Greek and Indic evidence, to say nothing of the later European stories of the *Bride Won in a Tournament*, it seems very likely that the versions of the chariot race for Hippodameia that feature Myrtilos predate Pindar's account. Preselection of the groom and manipulation of the contest to arrange his victory seem to be a common element in this type of story, and must have been so even in very distant antiquity. Pindar must have employed a version of the legend that featured a different configuration of the story's inherited motifs, like the legends of the contests for Sītā and for Damayantī recorded in the *Rāmāyaṇa* and *Mahābhārata*.

I say that he employed a different version rather than that he innovatively suppressed an element of the story for two reasons. First, I believe in the general principle that we should not assume an apparent mythic variant to be an actual innovation without good evidence that it did not exist earlier in a way that simply evades our evidence.[34] Second, the disparity between the two main versions of the race accords very well with what one would expect of legends passed down in an oral tradition, as this legend should be assumed to have been throughout most of its history prior to Pindar. Such was one of the most important discoveries of Parry and Lord's famous studies in South Slavic epic song.[35] In these investigations it was evident that individual legends, as they occurred in various songs, were rarely presented in a consistent way from performance to performance. Even when the same myth was related by the same performer on multiple occasions it would appear in varying form. When multiple performances of similar myths were compared, however, networks of commonly linked narratological elements emerged that were quite persistent, just as is the case here. No two council scenes were ever the same, for example, even when they supposedly described the exact same council. Nevertheless, all council scenes drew from the same broad set of narratological elements.[36] It is through familiarity with such sets of thematically linked narratological elements that performers remember and perform complex mythological narratives. A singer does not have to perform a canonical version of a myth, but instead to deploy elements of the proper broad thematic model. That is to say, the performer does not necessarily think of how a particular myth goes, but about how myths of that sort tend to go. In such traditions the omission of particular motifs from individual performances is expected, as is altering of motif according to performers' creativity and ability to adapt motifs familiar from other story-types. Some such modifications eventually prove more popular or useful than others and become influential traditions on their own. This yields a complex, fluid array of narratological traditions and a polymorphic, living mythic landscape.

We, of course, cannot study the innumerable times that this story must have been performed in archaic Greece to determine the sorts of variations to which the story was subject, but we can approximate this sort of analysis by

---

[34] See also Nagy 1990b:118.
[35] Lord 2000:68–123.
[36] See especially Lord 2000:79–96.

comparing it to the various choosing-ceremonies from Greek and Indic legend. Such a comparison shows that the versions of the race for Hippodameia that feature cheating, although they themselves come from later texts, did not articulate a later version of the myth, but one that simply illustrates a different configuration of the inherited narratological elements that make up a choosing-ceremony tale.[37]

This evidence should influence our understanding of Penelope's actions at the close of *Odyssey* XIX, since the precise timing and motivation of Penelope's decision to hold the bow contest is famously perplexing (as indicated by the question marks in the tables presented above).[38] After delaying her remarriage for so long, why does she hold the contest only after she receives the first real signs that Odysseus may be back soon, both from the disguised Odysseus himself and from a portentous dream? It has often been suggested that Penelope held the contest because she already had some knowledge that the beggar was Odysseus. It has been proposed that what we have in our text results from an earlier *Odyssey* in which Penelope was explicitly aware of the beggar's identity,[39] or that Penelope has simply seen through his disguise and has not let on.[40] It seems more likely, however, that the phenomena that shaped the story of the choosing-ceremony of Penelope are the same as those that shaped the contest for Hippodameia.[41] Both employ several narratological elements attendant to the choosing-ceremony tradition and both must have existed in a polymorphic

---

[37] It is not difficult to find other subjects in Greek myth that could demonstrate this phenomenon as well. The most prominent Artemis myths, for example (Actaeon, Callisto, Iphigenia), all draw from the same nexus of elements: violations of chastity, animal transformations, and ironic death. Variations within these individual mythic traditions (e.g. the fact that the stories of Actaeon and Iphigenia sometimes involve animal transformations, or substitutions, and sometimes do not) may reflect the same sort of variation seen in the myth of Hippodameia's choosing-ceremony.

[38] Levaniouk offers a thorough analysis of the interactions between Penelope and the disguised Odysseus, with an eye toward this very question, i.e. does Penelope recognize Odysseus? Levaniouk shows compellingly how Penelope's seemingly perplexing responses to Odysseus may best be seen as clever and fitting rhetorical strategy (2011:195–228). For an overview and evaluation of varied approaches to this problems see Combellack 1973:32–40; Heubeck 1988:III.104–105.

[39] Kirk 1962:246–247; Page 1955:123–126.

[40] Austin 1975:230–232; Harsh 1950:1–21; Amory 1963:100–121.

[41] The influences highlighted here are not the only ones that may be at work in the Odyssean bow-ceremony, and other comparanda may be relevant without requiring revision of the current hypothesis. On the relationship of this scene to Indian kingship rituals, which also involve bows, see Jamison 1999. Egyptian parallels have been adduced as well, and I see no reason to reject them; see Walcot 1984:357–369. Even though this story owes much of its genealogy to IE tradition, complimentary traditions from other nonrelated but influential cultures may also have had an impact. Interesting parallels in the Ugarit *Aqhat* have also been discussed by Ready (2010:155–157).

mythic landscape prior to, and perhaps alongside, our literary tradition. That is to say that various recountings of it should have been shaped by the same nexus of thematic elements, but may not have been limited to one configuration of those elements. It is the type of story in which the rigging of the contest on behalf of a pre-chosen winner is a common element, and so variants of this type may well have existed. Just as in *Olympian* I, the absence of explicit rigging in our Homeric text may simply reflect the privileging of one configuration of tradition elements among many other existent, if less successful, configurations.[42]

This explanation accounts for the variations in cheating in our main sources for the contest for Hippodameia, but does not address the Killos version discussed by Hansen or the relationship of this story to later European folktales. The folktale tradition to which those are connected, the *Bride Won in a Tournament*, features some of the same motifs that the Greek and Indic parallels would lead us to expect. There is a gathering of men to sue for the right to marry a young woman, there is a contest to choose the winner, and there is help from an unexpected person that proves decisive in the hero's victory. The contest, however, never involves archery, there is no rigging as such, and there is no disguise (except that the hero often wears the equipment of the helper).

Despite these differences, all of these versions may still descend from the same tradition of choosing-ceremony tales, because that story-type must itself have been multiform in its origin. Even among the speakers of PIE, the contest motif must have allowed for variation in the type of contest employed. Bow contests and horse races seem particularly natural expressions of this motif for PIE culture, so they may have been particularly common. These then were both influential in later traditions, but the fact they are not equally important in all subsequent traditions poses no real problem. While the version of this motif that employs bow contests may have disappeared from medieval and Renaissance stories, chariot racing and bow contests were both clearly preserved in Greek and Indic tales. A fourth tradition also seems to have been preserved, or perhaps invented, in Greece in the form of a footrace, documented in the contest to marry Atalanta and in the race that Odysseus won when he

---

[42] I have not included here every choosing-ceremony in Greece and India, but those that seemed to me most relevant to Pindar's account of the choosing-ceremony of Hippodameia. A few of those unmentioned do, however, contain at least a possibility of rigging as well. In the *Mahābhārata* Ambā is abducted from her choosing-ceremony and complains to her abductor that she had already chosen the man who should have won the contest (*Mahābhārata* V.170ff.). Additionally, the gathering of the suitors for Helen described in the Hesiodic catalogue indicates that Odysseus never sent gifts to woo Helen because he already knew that Menelaus was going to win (Solmsen 1990:198.4–6). For possible examples of other scenes in Greek myth see Schmidt 1987:94–96.

first married Penelope.[43] The identity of the unexpected helper must also have varied, at times being a stranger and at other times a person associated with the contest, in which case preselection of the winner and rigging of the contest would have been involved. Finally, the use of disguise could easily have been only an occasional element. The privileging of various expressions and configurations of these motifs could eventually lead to such traditions as those seen in Renaissance and medieval Europe, as well as those in ancient Greece and India.

Traditional approaches to Pindar's treatment of Myrtilos in *Olympian* I propose two mutually exclusive possibilities: that Pindar suppressed the involvement of Myrtilos, or that he was unaware of it (perhaps because it was not yet part of the tradition). Comparative evidence, however, shows such a proposition to be too simplistic. The consistency of the nexus of narrative elements that make up choosing-ceremony tales, both in Greece and elsewhere in the IE world, makes it difficult to imagine that the involvement of Myrtilos is not a very ancient element of the story. This, however, does not necessarily mean that Pindar simply suppressed the detail. The processes of mythopoesis make it likely that multiple versions of this story coexisted with each other, differing in their configuration of the elements of the choosing-ceremony theme. Pindar simply chose a preexistent version of the story that suited his immediate needs. Ultimately, the relationship of Pindar's account of the race to later versions proves less important than the relationship of these two versions to the wide range of choosing-ceremony stories in IE literature. It is in this relationship that we catch a glimpse of the story's PIE ancestry as well as the mythopoetic mechanisms that connect that ancestry to the literature of medieval and Renaissance Europe, as well as to the great epics of Greece and India.

To apply these findings to the myth of the Aśvins and its relationship to the myth of Pelops and Hippodameia we do not need to ask whether these two myths descend from one original chariot myth at all, but whether they take part in elements of the same inherited mythopoetic tradition of the choosing-ceremony, a tradition that featured a contest, the use of special equipment, disguise, and rigging. I believe that they do.

The fact that the Aśvins were believed to have obtained their wife in a contest is clear enough from the texts themselves, as well from the work of Jamison, and the special nature of that equipment is also easily shown. The chariot of the Aśvins was perhaps the most unusual and magnificent of all divine chariots in Indian mythology. It was fashioned and given to them by the Ṛbhus, the divine craftsmen, children of Tvaṣṭṛ, the premiere divine craftsman

---

[43] Pausanias III 12.2.

(*Ṛgveda* I.20.3; IV.33.8; X.39.12), it is of prodigious size (*Ṛgveda* VII.69.1), and is alone among chariots in possessing three wheels (*Ṛgveda* I.34.9; IV.36.1; X.41.1).[44] Their horses are also famously swift, although this is true generally of the horses of the gods. They were also winged, as shown above.[45]

Regarding the remaining criteria, disguise and rigging, our texts provide us with only the most tantalizing bits of evidence. *Ṛgveda* X.85 describes the marriage of Sūryā, but is famously unorthodox and very difficult to follow. This hymn is odd because it calls the Aśvins the wooers (*varā*, 8, 9), but identifies the groom as Soma, the deity and divine drink that was central in Indo-Iranian ritual cult, and from whose use the Aśvins were once prohibited (*somo vadhūyurabhavad*, "Soma was the groom" [9]). It seems as if we are seeing here evidence of two traditions, one in which the Aśvins won the race and one in which they lost to Soma, a deity of superior rank and of whom they were once judged unworthy. Several of our choosing-ceremony myths involve seemingly inferior contestants winning unexpectedly, so perhaps we have here details suggesting that the victory of the Aśvins in our texts was not the only or most expected outcome of the contest. This is very speculative, of course, but proof that this myth is related to the other choosing-ceremony myths does not require that they exhibit every feature of the complex after all, but only some, and we do have that here, even if certain details of the myth are unclear and require speculation.

The fact that chariots were common in IE cultures but not in the parent culture means that in investigating equine poetics within the IE communities we will occasionally encounter similarities in treatment that frustrate our understanding of the history of the chariot. In these situations, it is important, I think, that we not simply ignore the archaeological evidence to allow ourselves easier answers, answers that allow for simple cognate relationship when we encounter similar chariot-based imagery. We must also remember that although the chariot itself is not a shared inheritance, much else is common inheritance among the daughter cultures, such as the poetic and intellectual treatment of horses, and the very narratological patterns of the cultures' mythologies. In the context of such fundamental cultural similarities it is not at all surprising that some of the innovations of the daughter cultures would develop in ways that

---

[44] Jhala's very useful book, *Aśvinā in the Rigveda*, points to further features still, such as its golden color and its wondrous contents (1978:73–80). *Ṛgveda* X.85.16 describes Sūryā herself having three wheels, one of which is hidden from all but those who understand reality. This three-wheeled car of Sūryā is, presumably, the chariot of the Aśvins.

[45] It is remarkable that the horses of the Aśvins and of Pelops, and in some traditions of Nala, were all winged. I do not know of any evidence that makes the phenomenon of winged horses an inherited tradition, so for the moment I consider this a coincidence.

are similar to each other. In the case of the chariot-based marriage contest, just as in the case of the metapoetic charioteer, we must be prepared to plumb IE cultural histories widely in order to recognize the complex and convoluted ways in which a cognate relationship manifests. To appreciate the effect of IE inheritance on poetic treatment of horses, then, we must be prepared at times to look even beyond the horses themselves, to the wide range of inherited phenomena that could affect their depictions.

Conclusion

To appreciate any literary subject it is best to know what came before. The scholar of Hellenistic poetry, for example, brings to bear on the subject a knowledge of Classical Greek literature and culture. Yet in the case of the earliest phases of Greek poetry we rarely have access to comparable information, so we are forced to approach the subject in a very different way. The point of this study has been to highlight ways to mitigate this problem, to find in comparative evidence a vantage point from which we can view our earliest Greek poetry in the light of its otherwise obscured past. Horses have been my particular subject because they are especially interesting, but also because they are especially fit for such analysis. There is enough evidence and scholarship concerning horses in the IE world that several facets of the subject can be discussed with unusual confidence. Central to this is the fact that horses were featured in poetry through an extremely ancient poetic expression that was preserved in three daughter languages, and that they were central to an important sacrificial ritual, which united the themes of hippomorphism and sex. They are also a prominent subject in early Greek poetry, where they are treated in certain special ways that, I think, reveal new meaning when viewed through this historical evidence.

My work began with the Homeric formula ὠκέες ἵπποι, which descended through a continuous chain of poetic performance from PIE antiquity to ancient Greece. My goal was first to highlight the poetic qualities of the phrase, both in sound and in meaning, in the poetry of the parent culture and then to explore how it was preserved and flourished in Greece. The phrase was remarkably euphonic in its original form and in fact remained so in Greek up until a time just prior to that captured by our texts. Its euphony, erstwhile significance as a *figura etymologica*, and eventual metrical utility in dactylic verse allowed it not only to survive into Greek but to proliferate there, modified and expanded in a wide range of Homeric formulas, variously and creatively deployed by the poets. Ultimately, this investigation led me to argue that the intriguing Homeric epithet of Hades, κλυτόπωλος, came into use as a result of the development of the network of formulas related to ὠκέες ἵπποι.

From formulas about horses I moved to horses themselves, and to their relationship to humans, particularly epic heroes. Horses have a special position in the world of early Greek verse, wherein they are uniquely similar to humans. This similarity extends beyond martial valor to the very level of ontology, as can be seen in the presence of immortal and semi-divine horses. The existence of such horses runs parallel to that of the semi-divine heroes and their own immortal parents. This similarity is part of a broad overlap of horse and hero that not only shaped Greek epic poetry at a very fundamental level but can be seen in related IE poetry, notably that of ancient India. In positing that these parallel phenomena spring from a tendency mutually inherited from the parent culture I looked to evidence yielded by the PIE horse sacrifice ritual. I avoided detailed reconstruction of that ritual in favor of a minimal schema, focusing only on evidence of the potential for humans and horses to represent each other on a ritualistic level. Such an approach is especially important in the study of Greek culture because Greece did not preserve such a ritual itself. Greece was, however, an inheritor of the ideology that had shaped it.

The ritual's specific linking of horse and human identity in the realm of sex was also explored, and I argued that the ritual testifies to a tendency in the parent culture to use horses as a tool through which to think about human sex and power. This broad tendency was used as a backdrop against which to read Greek lyric depictions of both male and female sexual figures who are themselves depicted as horses. The connection between horses and sex also led to an investigation of the sexual connotations of the word *menos*, and its verbal root *men-, to which horses are often connected in Greece and elsewhere. Not only is the word of surprisingly wide semantic range, but so is its root, having throughout the IE languages meanings having to do with thought, physical strength, sex, and the production of poetry. In this final sphere, that of poetry, the connection between horses, sex, and humans is especially interesting, because it may, I have suggested, help to explain the origin of the metapoetic charioteer, a figure observable in several IE poetic traditions. The fact that charioteering cannot itself be traced to the parent culture means that the appearance of this figure in multiple daughter cultures should not be explained as a simple common inheritance. I suggested that this figure developed independently in the distinct traditions through the commonly inherited symbology of the horse and its connections to μένος. I argue that the verbal root *men- should be understood to mean something like "to direct one's life force" in a way that could produce valorous acts, sexual acts, or acts of intellectual production like poetry. In this concept I see a link between horses, heroes, and poets that helped shape the development of the metapoetic charioteer.

A difficulty raised by the metapoetic charioteer led to the final subject of my work, namely what to do with similarities in treatment of horses across the IE world that cannot be traced directly to the parent culture. My specific concern was the multiple occurrences of chariots in marriage myths, and I argued, as I had in the previous section, that similarities in cultural background can lead to parallel developments subsequent to the dispersal of the daughter cultures. In this case, however, I do not see the pertinent inherited material in horses per se but in the mythopoetic structure of the marriage ritual. Specifically I look at the marriage race for Hippodameia as told in Pindar's *Olympian I* and argue that marriage ritual myths elsewhere in Greece and India document an inherited network of mythopoetic techniques for the depiction of marriage contests, of which the chariot race myth is simply one variety, independently created in multiple traditions.

I have not, of course, investigated every facet of early Greek poetic treatment of horses. I expect, in fact, that even in the realm of inherited equine poetics subjects remain that could profitably expand this investigation. I hope, however, that I have made meaningful inroads into this study and usefully mapped out paths around common obstacles. I will be very happy if in so doing I have also drawn attention to this fascinating and elusive element of early Greek verse.

Appendix

Centaurs

It is difficult to discuss horses and hippomorphism in Greece without mentioning the figure of the centaur, so I will not conclude this work without doing so. There is no real reason to suspect that the figure is of IE origin, and its treatment is different from that of horses themselves, yet some traces of the IE equine ideology outlined above may still be observable in it.[1] They evince something of the heroic and sexual force seen in the horse elsewhere, but the centaurs' expression of that force is remarkably violent, and almost universally male.

A note on the shape of the centaur is necessary, since they are not always depicted in the form with which we are most familiar. Our earliest references involve no real description at all. Observe the evidence from both the *Iliad* and the *Homeric Hymn to Hermes*:

κάρτιστοι μὲν ἔσαν καὶ καρτίστοις ἐμάχοντο
φηρσὶν ὀρεσκῷοισι καὶ ἐκπάγλως ἀπόλεσσαν.

They were very brave men, and they did battle with the very brave mountain-dwelling [centaurs] and destroyed them terribly.

Iliad I 267–268

---

[1] Centaurs have occasionally been linked to the Indian *gandharvas*, celestial beings who have partially animalistic forms. The similarities in the names makes this connection tempting, but an etymological link is simply not present. Although the sounds are similar, there is no reason to expect the Greek unvoiced velar stop (the *k* sound) to have a counterpart in the Sanskrit voiced velar (the *g* sound), nor is there any reason, in this word, for the Greek unvoiced, unaspirated dental stop (the *t* sound) to have a counterpart in the Sanskrit voiced, aspirated stop (the *dh* sound). On the possibility that folk etymology could be hindering our recognition of an etymological relationship, MacDonnel (1898:137) cites numerous mythologically based objections. For a comparative analysis of centaurs generally and the difficulty of analyzing them comparatively see Dumézil 1929.

βήματα δ' οὔτ' ἀνδρὸς τάδε γίγνεται οὔτε γυναικὸς
οὔτε λύκων πολιῶν οὔτ' ἄρκτων οὔτε λεόντων·
οὔτε τι κενταύρου λασιαύχενος ἔλπομαι εἶναι
ὅς τις τοῖα πέλωρα βιβᾷ ποσὶ καρπαλίμοισιν·

These are not the footprints of a man or woman, or of hoary wolves or
bears or lions, nor do I think these are from a shaggy centaur, whoever
makes such monstrous footprints with swift feet.

Homeric Hymn to Hermes 222–225

The best early evidence from which we can draw any real conclusions comes
from material art, which represents some centaurs with human feet and geni-
tals in the front.[2] These are depicted as part horse, and thus roughly correspond
to the classical model, even if they are not precisely what one might expect. It
has been suggested that these were late models, which represent evolutions of
a centaur form that was not hippomorphic at all.[3] Even if this is the case, it is
still clear that the hippomorphic form of the centaur was eventually standard-
ized and must have made sense to the Greeks with respect to other aspects of
the centaurs' mythology and Greece's equine ideology more generally. Thus it
remains reasonable to look to centaurs for evidence of Greek attitudes toward
horses.

As in the case of the IE horse the association between centaurs and sexuality is very common, but in the case of the centaurs that sex is almost always
violent. The most famous example stems from the myth of Nessos attempting
to rape Deianeira, depicted by the Nessos Painter, in Sophocles' *Trachiniai*, and
elsewhere.[4] Nessos not only attempted to rape Deianeira but then convinced her
that a mixture of his blood and semen would serve as a love charm to secure the
affections of Heracles, which it did not. A connection between centaurs, sexual
assault, and semen is also demonstrated by Nonnos, who incorporates this motif
into his depiction of horned centaurs sprung from the semen of Zeus:

... ὁππότε Κύπρις ἐπέτρεχεν εἴκελος αὔραις
ἴχνιον ἱμείροντος ἀλυσκάζουσα τοκῆος,
μὴ γενέτην ἀθέμιστον ἐσαθρήσειεν ἀκοίτην,
Ζεὺς δὲ πατὴρ ὑπόειξε γάμων ἄψαυστον ἐάσσας
ὠκυτέρην ἀκίχητον ἀναινομένην Ἀφροδίτην·
ἀντὶ δὲ Κυπριδίων λεχέων ἔσπειρεν ἀρούρῃ

---

[2] See Arnold 1973.
[3] Harrison 1980:382–385.
[4] *Trachiniae* 555–581; Apollodorus *Bibliotheca* II 7.6; Diodorus Siculus IV 36.

παιδογόνων προχέων φιλοτήσιον ὄμβρον ἀρότρων·
γαῖα δὲ δεξαμένη γαμίην Κρονίωνος ἐέρσην
ἀλλοφυῆ κερόεσσαν ἀνηκόντιζε γενέθλην.

Once Cypris [Aphrodite] ran like the winds fleeing the pursuit of her amorous father, so that she might not see an unlawful fatherly bedmate, and her father Zeus gave up his pursuit of the union, leaving untouched the swifter, unattainable, and unwilling Aphrodite. Instead of the bed of Aphrodite, he ejaculated on the earth, pouring forth the love-shower of child-producing plows. The earth received the marital dew of the son of Cronos and hurled forth the strange horned race.

Nonnos *Dionysiaca* XIV 194–202

Like the centaur, the sexual symbolism of the PIE horse and the Greek horse thereafter is also intimately connected to erotic power and with semen, but the centaur exhibits this connection in a particularly extreme and violent form.

The myth of the wedding of Peirithoos is another well-documented example of the violent sexual nature of centaur mythology. This wedding is said to have led to the famous battle of the Lapiths and Centaurs, which is frequently depicted in literature and which is an important enough artistic motif to appear on the Parthenon, the Hephaisteion, and the temple to Zeus at Olympia. At this wedding the centaur Eurytion attempted to rape the bride, and the other centaurs followed by attempting to rape the other women and boys in attendance.[5]

Even the story of the centaurs' creation links the figures essentially with extreme and inappropriate sexual impulse. Pindar's *Pythian* II tells of how Ixion was brought by Zeus to Olympus, where it was discovered that Ixion intended to have sex with Hera. Zeus was in disbelief, so tested Ixion by fashioning an eidolon, or copy, of Hera, like that fashioned of Helen, and Ixion did indeed have sex with it. From this union was born a man named Kentauros, who had sex with the mares around Mount Pelion, and from them the race of the centaurs was born.[6] For his act Ixion was punished by being tied eternally to a spinning chariot wheel. Since chariot wheels spin due to the force of horses this form of punishment is ironic. The eternally spinning wheel reflects unchecked equine force because Ixion's own sexual impulses were incontrollable, and the eventual

---

[5] Diodorus Siculus IV 70.3–4; Pausanias V 10.8; Plutarch *Life of Theseus* 30.3. It is perhaps significant that the bride at this ceremony was Hippodamia, the horse tamer. This is not the same Hippodamia who was discussed in Chapter 4, the wife of Pelops, but it does seem that in both instances the name of the woman is particularly well suited to the myth.

[6] *Pythian* II 40–50.

and logical product of that sexual impulse was the race of the centaurs. The centaurs' very essence is linked to a sexual impulse associated with horses, but the centaurs' expression of it is uniquely violent and transgressive.

Unlike Greek mythological horses, however, the centaur is almost always male, as confirmed by a story about Zeuxis told by Lucian. In it Lucian describes a painting of a female centaur done by Zeuxis and compliments it not only because of its quality, but because of the ingenuity involved in contriving something so very novel:

Ἐθέλω γοῦν ὑμῖν καὶ τὸ τοῦ γραφέως διηγήσασθαι. ὁ Ζεῦξις ἐκεῖνος ἄριστος γραφέων γενόμενος τὰ δημώδη καὶ τὰ κοινὰ ταῦτα οὐκ ἔγραφεν, ἢ ὅσα πάνυ ὀλίγα, ἥρωας ἢ θεοὺς ἢ πολέμους, ἀεὶ δὲ καινοποιεῖν ἐπειρᾶτο καί τι ἀλλόκοτον ἂν καὶ ξένον ἐπινοήσας ἐπ' ἐκείνῳ τὴν ἀκρίβειαν τῆς τέχνης ἐπεδείκνυτο. ἐν δὲ τοῖς ἄλλοις τολμήμασι καὶ θήλειαν Ἱπποκένταυρον ὁ Ζεῦξις οὗτος ἐποίησεν, ἀνατρέφουσάν γε προσέτι παιδίω Ἱπποκενταύρω διδύμω κομιδῇ νηπίω.

I want to give you an example from a painter. Zeuxis, that most excellent of painters, did not depict popular or common themes (heroes, gods, or wars, for example) but always endeavored to create novelty, and when he created something new and unusual he demonstrated the precision of his skill. Among his daring works, this Zeuxis created a female centaur, one who, moreover, nursed twin centaur children, babies.[7]

Zeuxis or Antiochus 3.1–10

Female centaurs seem to have rarely entered the Greek imagination.[8] We saw in Chapter 3 that in Greece equine characterizations of humans are deployed along strictly gendered lines: men are compared to horses in their sexual impulse and power while women are compared to horses in their need to be broken and tamed. The unruliness and incivility of the centaur are used in Greek myth to represent that which is wild and essentially uncontrollable, a purpose to which the symbolic connection between horses and men is apparently more fit than

---

[7] The exact same motif was exploited by early animator Winsor McCay in his short animated piece, "The Centaurs," from 1921. The novelty and fantastic potential of the medium of animation was exemplified in the depiction not only of centaurs, who could not at that time be realistically depicted in other media, but by the depiction of a female centaur and children. In 1940 Walt Disney did likewise in his animated work, "Fantasia," by presenting female centaurs called centaurettes.

[8] Representations of them are not, however, entirely unknown. For example, the Pella Archaeological Museum houses a fourth-century mosaic depicting a female centaur.

that between horses and women; hence female centaurs are ignored except as an occasional novelty.

It is useful to dwell for a moment on the anomalous centaur, Chiron, the legendary trainer of Achilles, about whom there is no story of violent sex. His character is entirely at odds with that of the other centaurs and he is, in fact, referred to as δικαιότατος κενταυρέων, "most just of centaurs."[9] Yet his birth is also consistently distinct from that of all other centaurs. Hesiod says that he is the child of Phillyra,[10] and other sources add that he is the child of Cronos who mated with this Phillyra, a daughter of Oceanos, while he had taken the form of horse.[11] It seems that Chiron is the exception that proves the rule: his civility was so unlike that of all other centaurs that an alternative genealogy was necessary.

Although he represents a particularly dangerous and uncontrollable expression of the forces discussed throughout this work, the centaur does, in a way, exhibit the same thematic nexus of hippomorphism, sex, and power that was seen in the hero. It is in this twisted manifestation of the very elements of heroic identity, expressed hippologically, that the centaur achieves his identity, a reflection of the hero that is nevertheless grotesquely anti-heroic.

---

[9] *Iliad* XI 832.
[10] *Theogony* 1001–1002.
[11] *Titanomachia* frag. 10 *Poetae Epici Graeci*; Pherekydes 3 F 50; cf. Ovid *Metamorphoses* VI 126.

Bibliography

Adrados, F. R. 2007. "The Panorama of Indo-European Linguistics since the Middle of the Twentieth Century: Advances and Immobilism." *Journal of Indo-European Studies* 35:129–153.

Albêrûnî. 2002. *Albêrûnî's India.* Trans. E. C. Sachau. New Delhi.

Allan, J. 1914. *Catalogue of the Coins of the Gupta Dynasties and of Śaśāṅka, King of Gauda.* London.

Amory, A. 1963. "The Reunion of Odyssey and Penelope." In *Essays on the Odyssey: Selected Modern Criticism,* ed. C. H. Taylor, 100–121. Bloomington.

Anderson, J. K. 1961. *Ancient Greek Horsemanship.* Berkeley.

Anthony, D. W. 1986. "The 'Kurgan Culture,' Indo-European Origins, and the Domestication of the Horse: A Reconsideration." *Current Anthropology* 27.4: 291–313.

———. 2007. *The Horse, the Wheel, and Language: How Bronze-Age Riders from the Eurasian Steppes Shaped the Modern World.* Princeton.

Arnold, R. 1973. *The Horse-Demon in Early Greek Art and His Eastern Neighbors.* New York.

Athanassakis, A. N. 2002. "Akhilleus's Horse Balios: Old and New Etymologies." *Glotta* 78:1–11.

Austin, N. 1975. *Archery at the Dark of the Moon: Poetic Problems in Homer's Odyssey.* Berkeley.

Balter, M. 2003. "Linguistics: Early Date for the Birth of Indo-European Languages." *Science* 302.5650:1490–1491.

Bassett, S. E. 1926. "The So-Called Emphatic Position of the Runover Word in the Homeric Hexameter." *Transactions and Proceedings of the American Philological Association* 57:116–148.

Beaumont, R. L. 1936. "Greek Influence in the Adriatic Sea before the Fourth Century B.C." *Journal of Hellenic Studies* 56:159–204.

Beekes, R. S. P. 1988. *A Grammar of Gatha-Avestan.* Leiden.

———. 2013. *Etymological Dictionary of Greek.* Leiden.

Blackburn, S. H. 1989. *Oral Epics in India.* Berkeley.

Bowra, C. M. 1961. *Heroic Poetry.* London.

Brockington, J. 1998. *The Sanskrit Epics*. Leiden.

Brooten, B. J. 1996. *Love between Women: Early Christian Responses to Female Homo-eroticism*. Chicago.

Burkert, W. 1983. *Homo Necans: The Anthropology of Ancient Greek Sacrificial Ritual and Myth*. Berkeley.

Camp, J. 1998. *Horses and Horsemanship in the Athenian Agora. Agora Picture Book 24*. Athens.

Campbell, D. A. 1967. *Greek Lyric Poetry: A Selection of Early Greek Lyric, Elegiac, and Iambic Poetry*. London.

Childe, V. G. 1926. *The Aryans: A Study of Indo-European Origins*. London.

Clackson, J. 1994. The Linguistic Relationship between Armenian and Greek. *Publications of the Philological Society 30*. Oxford.

Combellack, F. M. 1973. "Three Odyssean Problems." *California Studies in Classical Antiquity* 6:17–46.

Cook, E. F. 1995. *The* Odyssey *in Athens: Myths of Cultural Origins*. Ithaca.

Danek, G. 1988. *Studien zur Dolonie*. Vienna.

Dawkins, R. M. 1929. *The Sanctuary of Artemis Orthia at Sparta*. London.

Delebecque, E. 1951. *Le cheval dans l'Iliade, suivi d'un lexique du cheval chez Homère et d'un essai sur le cheval préhomérique*. Paris.

Dent, A. A. 1974. *The Horse through Fifty Centuries of Civilization*. New York.

Doniger O'Flaherty, W. D. 1980. *Women, Androgynes, and Other Mythical Beasts*. Chicago.

Dover, K. J. 1977. *Greek Homosexuality*. Cambridge.

Drews, R. 1988. *The Coming of the Greeks: Indo-European Conquests in the Aegean and the Near East*. Princeton.

Dumézil, G. 1929. *Le problème des Centaures: Étude de mythologie comparée indo-européenne*. Paris.

———. 1954. *Rituels indo-européens à Rome. Études et commentaires 19*. Paris.

———. 1966. *La religion romaine archaïque*. Paris.

Dumont, P. É. 1927. *L'Ashvamedha: Description du sacrifice solennel du cheval dans le culte védique d'après les textes du Yajurveda blanc (Vajasaneyisamhita, Shatapathabrahmana, Katyayanasrautasutra)*. Paris.

Durante, M. 1971. *Sulla preistoria della tradizione poetica greca*. Rome.

Edwards, A. T. 1988. "*Kleos Aphthiton* and Oral Theory." *Classical Quarterly* 38:25–30.

Edwards, M. W. 1991. *The Iliad: A Commentary, V: Books 17–20*. Ed. G. S. Kirk. Cambridge.

Egoscozábal, C. 2003. "Los animales del «Yambo de las mujeres» de Semónides." *Estudios Classicos* 123:7–25.

Farnell, L. R. 1977. *The Cults of the Greek States*. New Rochelle.

Finkelberg, M. 1986. "Is *Kleos Aphthiton* a Homeric Formula?" *Classical Quarterly* 36:1–5.

Fisker, D. 1990. *Pindars erste Olympische Ode.* Odense.

Floyd, E. D. 1980. *"Kleos Aphthiton:* An Indo-European Perspective on Early Greek Poetry." *Glotta* 58:133–157.

Fontenrose, J. E. 1978. *The Delphic Oracle: Its Responses and Operations.* Berkeley.

Fortson, B. W. 2009. *Indo-European Language and Culture: An Introduction.* Malden.

Frame, D. 2009. *Hippota Nestor.* Hellenic Studies 37. Washington, DC.

Frisk, H. 1960. *Griechisches Etymologisches Wörterbuch I. 2 vols.* Heidelberg.

———. 1970. *Griechisches Etymologisches Wörterbuch II.* Heidelberg.

Fuchs, S. 1996. *The Vedic Horse Sacrifice in Its Culture-Historical Relations.* New Delhi.

Gamkrelidze, T. V., and V. V. Ivanov. 1995. *Indo-European and the Indo-Europeans.* Trans. J. Nichols. New York.

Gantz, T. 1993. *Early Greek Myth: A Guide to Literary and Artistic Sources.* Baltimore.

Georgiadou, A. 1997. *Plutarch's Pelopidas: A Historical and Philological Commentary.* Stuttgart.

Gerber, D. E. 1982. *Pindar's Olympian One: A Commentary.* Toronto.

Gimbutas, M. 1961. "Notes on the Chronology and Expansion of the Pit-Grave Culture." In *L'Europe à la fin de l'âge de pierre,* ed. J. Bohm and S. Laet, 193–200. Prague.

———. 1997. *The Kurgan Culture and the Indo-Europeanization of Europe: Selected Articles from 1952 to 1993.* Ed. M. R. Dexter and K. Jones-Bley. Washington, DC.

Gregory, J. A. 2007. "Donkeys and the Equine Heirarchy in Archaic Greek Literature." *Classical Journal* 102.3:193–212.

Gresseth, G. K. 1979. "The *Odyssey* and the *Nalopakhyana.*" *Transactions of the American Philological Association* 109:63–85.

Griffith, M. 2006. "Horsepower and Donkeywork: Equids and the Ancient Greek Imagination. Part Two." *Classical Philology* 101.4:307–358.

Haak, W., et al. 2015. "Massive Migration from the Steppe Was a Source for Indo-European Languages in Europe." *Nature* 522:207–211.

Hainsworth, J. B. 1968. *The Flexibility of the Homeric Formula.* Oxford.

———. 1969. *Homer. Greece & Rome* 3. Oxford.

Hamp, E. P. 1990. "Pre-Indo-European Language of Northern (Central) Europe." In *When Worlds Collide: The Indo-Europeans and the Pre-Indo-Europeans,* ed. T. L. Markey and J. A. C. Greppin, 291–309. Ann Arbor.

Hansen, W. F. 2000. "The Winning of Hippodameia." *Transactions of the American Philological Association* 130:19–40.

———. 2002. *Ariadne's Thread: A Guide to International Tales Found in Classical Literature, Myth, and Poetics.* Ithaca.

Harrison, J. E. 1980. *Prolegomena to the Study of Greek Religion*. London.

Harsh, P. 1950. "Penelope and Odysseus in *Odyssey* XIX." *American Journal of Philology* 71:1–21.

Heubeck, A., S. West, J. B. Hainsworth, and A. Hoekstra. 1988. *A Commentary on Homer's* Odyssey. Oxford.

Horrocks, G. C. 1980. "The Antiquity of the Greek Epic Tradition: Some New Evidence." *Proceedings of the Cambridge Philosophical Society* 206:1–11.

———. 1987. "The Ionian Epic Tradition: Was There an Aeolic Phase in Its Development?" *Minos* 20:269–294.

Hude, C. 1927. *Herodoti Historiae*. Oxford.

Hughes, D. D. 1991. *Human Sacrifice in Ancient Greece*. London.

Jamison, S. 1996. *Sacrificed Wife/Sacrificer's Wife: Women, Ritual, and Hospitality in Ancient India*. New York.

———. 1999. "Penelope and the Pigs: Indic Perspectives on the *Odyssey*." *Classical Antiquity* 18.2:227–272.

———. 2001. "The Rigvedic *Svayamvara*? Formulaic Evidence." In *Vidyarnava-vandanam: Essays in Honour of Asko Parpola*, ed. K. Karttunen and P. Koskikallio, 303–315. Helsinki.

———. 2003. "*Vedic* vra: Evidence for the *Svayamvara* in the *Rig Veda*?" In *Paiti-mana: Essays in Iranian, Indo-European, and Indian Studies in Honor of Hanns-Peter Schmidt*, ed. S. Adhami, 39–56. Costa Mesa.

Janko, R. 1982. *Homer, Hesiod, and the Hymns: Diachronic Development in Epic Diction*. Cambridge.

———. 1994. *The* Iliad*: A Commentary, IV: Books 13–16*. Ed. G. S. Kirk. Cambridge.

Jhala, G. 1978. *Aśvinā in the Rigveda*. Bombay.

Johnston, S. I. 1992. "Xanthus, Hera, and the Erinyes (*Iliad* 19.400–418)." *Transactions of the American Philological Association* 122:85–98.

Kakridis, J. 1930. "Die Pelopssage bei Pindar." *Philologus* 85:463–477.

Kammenhuber, A. 1961. *Hippologia Hethitica*. Wiesbaden.

Katz, J. T. 2010. "Inherited Poetics." In *A Companion to the Ancient Greek Language*, ed. E. J. Bakker, 357–369. Malden.

Kirk, G. S. 1962. *The Songs of Homer*. Cambridge.

———. 1990. *The* Iliad*: A Commentary*. Cambridge.

Kloekhorst, A. 2008. *Etymological Dictionary of the Hittite Inherited Lexicon*. Leiden.

Köhnken, A. 1974. "Pindar as Innovator: Poseidon Hippios and the Relevance of the Pelops Story in *Olympian* 1." *Classical Quarterly* 24:199–206.

Koppers, W. 1936. *Pferdeopfer und Pferdekult der Indogermanen: Eine Ethnologisch-Religionswissenschaftliche Studie*. Salzburg.

Kosmetatou, E. 1993. "Horse Sacrifices in Greece and Cyprus." *Journal of Prehistoric Religion* 7:31–41.

Lacroix, L. 1976. "La légende de Pélops et son iconographie." *Bulletin de Correspondance Hellénique* 100:327–341.

Latona, M. 2008. "The Reigning In of the Passions: The Allegorical Interpretation of Parmenides B Fragment 1." *American Journal of Philology* 129.2:199–230.

Latte, K. 1966. *Hesychii Alexandri Lexicon II.* Copenhagen.

Levaniouk, O. 2011. *The Eve of the Festival.* Cambridge.

Liddel, H. G., R. Scott, and H. S. Jones. 1996. *A Greek-English Lexicon.* Oxford.

Lindsay, W. M. 1913. *Sexti Pompei Festi de Verborum Significatu quae Supersunt cum Pauli Epitome.* Leipzig.

Lord, A. B. 2000. *The Singer of Tales.* 2nd ed. Ed. S. A. Mitchell and G. Nagy. Cambridge.

Macdonell, A. A. 1898. *Vedic Mythology.* Strassburg.

Macurdy, G. H. 1923. "The Horse-Taming Trojans." *Classical Quarterly* 17.1:50–52.

Maehler, H. 1975. *Pindari Carmina cum Fragmentis.* Leipzig.

Mallory, J. P. 1981. "The Ritual Treatment of the Horse in the Early Kurgan Tradition." *Journal of Indo-European Studies* 9:205–226.

———. 1989. *In Search of the Indo-Europeans: Language, Archaeology, and Myth.* London.

———. 1993. "The Indo-European Homeland Problem—A Matter of Time." *Journal of Indo-European Studies Monograph* 17:1–22.

Mallory, J. P., and D. Q. Adams. 2006. *The Oxford Introduction to Proto-Indo-European and the Proto-Indo-European World.* Oxford.

Maringer, J. 1981. "The Horse in Art and Ideology of Indo-European Peoples." *Journal of Indo-European Studies* 9:177–204.

Markman, S. D. 1943. *The Horse in Greek Art.* Baltimore.

Martin, R. P. 1989. *The Language of Heroes: Speech and Performance in the Iliad.* Ithaca.

Matasovic, R. 1996. *A Theory of Textual Reconstruction in Indo-European Linguistics.* Frankfurt.

Meillet, A. 1897. *De Indo-Europaea radice *men- "mente agitare."* Paris.

Mirashi, V. V. 1963. *Corpus Inscriptionum Indicarum.* Ootacamund.

Moulton, C. 1977. *Similes in the Homeric Poems.* Hypomnemata 49. Göttingen.

Muellner, L. 1996. *The Anger of Achilles: Mēnis in Greek Epic.* Ithaca.

Nagler, M. N. 1967. "Towards a Generative View of Oral Formula." *Transactions of the American Philological Association* 98:269–311.

Nagy, G. 1974. *Comparative Studies in Greek and Indic Meter.* Cambridge.

———. 1990a. *Greek Mythology and Poetics.* Ithaca.

———. 1990b. *Pindar's Homer: The Lyric Possession of an Epic Past.* Baltimore.

Negelein, J. V. 1903. *Das Pferd im arischen Altertum.* Königsberg.

Nilsson, M. P. 1941. *Geschichte der griechischen Religion.* Munich.

Noonan, J. D. 2006. "Mettius Fufetius in Livy." *Classical Antiquity* 25.2:327–349.

O'Meara, J. J. 1949. "Giraldus Cambrensis in *Topographia Hibernie*. 'Text of the First Recension.'" *Proceedings of the Royal Irish Academy. Section C: Archaeology, Celtic Studies, History, Linguistics, Literature* 52:113–178.

Özgüç, T. 1988. *İnandıktepe: Eski hitit çağında önemli bir kült merkezi.* Ankara.

Page, D. L. 1951. *The Partheneion.* Oxford.

———. 1955. *The Homeric* Odyssey. Oxford.

———. 1973. *Folktales in Homer's Odyssey.* Cambridge.

Palmer, L. R., A. M. Davies, and W. Meid. 1976. *Studies in Greek, Italic, and Indo-European Linguistics.* Innsbruck.

Paraskevaides, H. A. 1984. *The Use of Synonyms in Homeric Formulaic Diction.* Amsterdam.

Pascal, C. B. 1981. "October Horse." *Harvard Studies in Classical Philology* 85:261–291.

Pischel, R., and K. F. Geldner. 1889. *Vedische Studien.* Stuttgart.

Platte, R. C. 2011. "Pindaric Mythopoesis." In *Proceedings of the 22nd Annual UCLA Indo-European Studies Conference.*

———. 2014. "Hades' Famous Foals and the Prehistory of Homeric Horse Formulas." *Oral Tradition* 29.1:149–162.

Pokorny, J. 1959. *Indogermanisches Etymologisches Wörterbuch.* Bern.

Pomeroy, S. B. 1975. *Goddesses, Whores, Wives, and Slaves: Women in Classical Antiquity.* New York.

Preisendanz, K. 1973. *Papyri Graecae Magicae: Die Greichischen Zauberpapyri.* Stuttgart.

Puhvel, J. 1955. "Vedic *áshvamedha-* and Gaulish *IIPOMIIDVOS.*" *Language* 31.3: 353–354.

———. 1978. "Victimal Hierarchies in Indo-European Animal Sacrifice." *American Journal of Philology* 99.3:354–362.

———. 1987. *Comparative Mythology.* Baltimore.

Ramachandran, T. N. 1951. "*Ashvamedha* Site near Kalsi." *Journal of Oriental Research* 21:1–31.

———. 1952. "The *Ashvamedha* Inscription near Kalsi: A Note." *Journal of Oriental Research* 22:100.

Raulwing, P. 2000. *Horses, Chariots, and Indo-Europeans.* Budapest.

Ready, J. 2010. "Why Odysseus Strings His Bow." *Greek, Roman, and Byzantine Studies* 50:133–157.

Rix, H. and M. Kümmel. 2001. *LIV - Lexikon der indogermanischen Verben: Die Wurzeln und ihre Primärstammbildungen.* Wiesbaden.

Robbins, E. 1994. "Alcman's *Partheneion*: Legend and Choral Ceremony." *Classical Quarterly* 44:7–16.

Russo, J. 2004. "Odysseus' Trial of the Bow as Symbolic Performance." In *Antike Literatur in neuer Deutung,* ed. A. Bierl, A. Schmitt, A. Willi, and J. Latacz, 95–102. Munich.

Rutherford, J. 2007. "My Little Calliponian." *Bitch* 35:19.

Salonen, A. 1956. *Hippologia Accadica.* Helsinki.

Schachter, A. 1981. *Cults of Boiotia.* London.

Schmidt, H. 1987. *Some Women's Rites and Rights in the Veda.* Poona.

Schmitt, R. 1967. *Dichtung und Dichtersprache in indogermanischer Zeit.* Wiesbaden.

Shapiro, H. A. 1994. *Myth into Art: Poet and Painter in Classical Greece.* London.

Sharma, R. S. 1993. "The Aryan Problem and the Horse." *Social Scientist* 21.7:3–16.

Sickle, J. V. 1975. "The New Erotic Fragment of Archilochus." *Quaderni Urbinati di Cultura Classica* 20:123–156.

Solmsen, F., R. Merkelbach, and M. L. West. 1990. *Hesiodi Theogonia; Opera et dies; Scutum.* Oxford.

Sparreboom, M. 1985. *Chariots in the Veda.* Leiden.

Thieme, P. 1968. "Hades." In *Indogermanische Dichtersprache,* ed. R. Schmitt, 133–153. Darmstadt.

Vaan, M. 2009. "The Derivational History of Greek ἵππος and ἱππεύς." *Journal of Indo-European Studies* 37:198–213.

Verrall, A. W. 1898. "Death and the Horse: κλυτόπωλος, κλυτός, ἕλιξ, etc." *Journal of Hellenic Studies* 18:1–14.

Volk, K. 2002. "*Kleos Aphthiton* Revisited." *Classical Philology* 97:61–88.

Walcot, P. 1984. "Odysseus and the Contest of the Bow: The Comparative Evidence." *Studi Micenei ed Egeo-Anatolici* 25:357–369.

Watkins, C. 1995. *How to Kill a Dragon.* Oxford.

West, M. L. 1988. "The Rise of Greek Epic." *Journal of Hellenic Studies* 108:151–172.

———. 1992. "The Descent of Greek Epic: A Reply." *Journal of Hellenic Studies* 112: 173–175.

———. 2007. *Indo-European Poetry and Myth.* Oxford.

Westlake, H. D. 1939. "The Sources of Plutarch's Pelopidas." *Classical Quarterly* 33.1: 11–22.

Witzel, M., and T. Goto. 2007. *Rig-Veda: Das heilige Wissen. Erster und zweiter Liederkreis.* Frankfurt.

Witzel, M., and S. Jamison. 2003. "Vedic Hinduism." In *The Study of Hinduism,* ed. A. Sharma, 65–113. Columbia, SC.

Woodard, R. D. 2006. *Indo-European Sacred Space: Vedic and Roman Cult.* Urbana.

Zirkle, C. 1936. "Animals Impregnated by the Wind." *Isis* 25.1:95–130.

Index of Ancient Sources

Please note: Page numbers followed by an italic *t* indicate a table.

Index of Mythological Figures

Please note: Page numbers followed by an italic *t* indicate a table.

Anglo-Saxon Mythology

Greek and Roman Mythology

Indian Mythology

Iranian Mythology

Lithuanian Mythology

Subject Index

Please note: Page numbers followed by an italic *t* indicate a table.